THE
COCKTAIL
BOOK

THE
COCKTAIL BOOK

CHANCELLOR
PRESS

Contents

The measure that has been used in the cocktail recipes is based on a bar jigger, which is 45 ml (1½ fl oz). If preferred, a different volume can be used providing the proportions are keep constant within a drink and suitable adjustments are made to spoon measures.

First published as *The Ultimate Cocktail Book*
in 2000 by Hamlyn, an imprint of
Octopus Publishing Group Ltd

This edition published 2002 by Chancellor Press,
an imprint of Bounty Books, a division of
Octopus Publishing Group Ltd
2-4 Heron Quays, London E14 4JP

Reprinted 2003, 2004

Copyright © 2000, 2001 Octopus Publishing Group Limited

ISBN 0-7537-0684-9
ISBN 13 9 780753 706848
Printed in China

INTRODUCTION

Cocktails are alcoholic mixed drinks, which are usually a mix-and-match concoction of at least two different liqueurs or spirits. They have enjoyed an enormous revival in fashion in recent years, with many exciting new cocktail bars opening.

Most of these cocktail bars offer a 'happy hour' in the early evening when drinks are half price – an added incentive that has no doubt added greatly to their popularity. So whereas cocktails were once drunk only on rare occasions, and then strictly before meals, this new availability has meant that people have adopted a more relaxed approach to them, and they are drunk nowadays as and when desired.

The range of delectable cocktails to choose from today is virtually endless – the rationale behind them being that they should offer a subtle and harmonious blend of flavours, as well as a powerful kick. It is always worth bearing this 'kick' in mind when you are offered a cocktail. They can slip down all too easily, and it is surprisingly simple to indulge in too many of them and end up rather the worse for wear. Many is the hangover that has been suffered the following day as a result of over-indulgence in cocktails – temptingly delicious but treacherously deadly!

Actually, it is worth knowing, while we're on the subject of hangovers, that the cocktails based on gin, vodka and white rum are actually lower in those dangerous constituents that are known to cause hangovers than the darker spirits. You have been warned!

History, origins and culture

The question of who invented the original cocktail is one that is asked by a great many people, and almost as many are convinced that they know the definitive answer. The problem is, however, that no two answers will ever be the same, and they can't all be right!

A great many people will come up without hesitation with the colourful story of Princess Xoctl, the Mexican princess who, according to legend, offered a drink to American officers at her father's court. A classic misunderstanding ensued; the soldiers thought that Xoctl was in fact the name of the drink rather than the princess's name. Thus the name cocktail passed into the history of drink as the name of a curiously exotic, lethally powerful and utterly delicious drink.

Unfortunately, this story probably owes more to a vivid imagination than to the truth, and the cocktail as we know it today almost certainly had its origins during the time of Prohibition in the United States in the 1920s, when alcohol was banned. The idea behind the cocktail was an attempt to create something drinkable out of the infamous bathtub gin and various

other bootlegged liquors. This was the time when furtive drinkers sat in the speakeasies of the day, eager to fool the authorities into believing that the drinks they were sipping from their tea cups were, in fact, free of forbidden hard liquor. Intent on their illegal purpose, they invented a fanciful coded system of imaginative and exciting names to disguise what was really in their cups. It was often these names that lent glamour, in part anyway, to the whole business of making, drinking and serving cocktails.

Prohibition began on 17 January 1920. It ended in December 1933 when, not surprisingly, the standard of the liquor that was available for sale improved beyond measure. This was a signal for many of the

better concoctions to become rather more refined. The full range of cocktails became more and more varied at this time, boasting more and more imaginative ingredients as well as more and more imaginative and fanciful names.

The cocktail really got into its stride as the range of cocktails increased, and cocktails became the drink that all the smart people liked to drink, not only in the US but also in all the more sophisticated cities of Britain and continental Europe. It wasn't long before every smart hotel and club in town could boast that it had a cocktail bar to its name.

The 1920s and 1930s were the golden age of the cocktail, and some of the more exotic ones that were formulated then are still drunk in bars today. The Bloody Mary, the Gimlet, the Tequila Sunrise, the Corpse Reviver, Buck's Fizz and the Zombie – these are all examples of drinks that were produced in the cocktail age of the '20s and '30s and that are still as popular among the smart set these days as they were then.

It may surprise you to learn, however, that some of the cocktails that we still enjoy today are, in fact, a lot older than that. Many cocktails have developed from the punches and cups that were fashionable so much earlier on, in the 18th and 19th centuries, when they were often served at public entertainments, parties and dances. The most famous cocktail of all time, for example, the Dry Martini, actually originated in the 19th century, though it has probably become steadily drier as tastes have changed – and people have become more sophisticated – over the years. The first-ever cocktail book went by the ponderous title of *The Bon Vivant's Guide, or How to Mix Drinks* by 'Professor' Jerry Thomas and was published in the United States as long ago as the 1860s. Many of the other classic cocktails, such as the Daiquiri, the Mint Julep and the Manhattan, also hail from those early days and were revived when cocktails enjoyed a come-back in the '20s and '30s.

There are other cocktails, too, such as the Harvey Wallbanger and the Piña Colada, which belong to the cocktail revival of the late '70s and early '80s. While others still, such as the B52 and other short, layered drinks known as shooters, served in a shot glass and intended to be downed in a single throw, are part of the very latest cocktail fashion.

Different types of cocktails
There are a great many different types of cocktail. A lot of them are based on spirits, but there are also many wine-based drinks and delicious alcohol-free cups based on fruit juices, teas and herbal teas. Cocktails were originally intended to be put together individually, according to each drinker's personal tastes and desires, which explains why the recipes for so many cocktails serve only one.

The fashion for the cocktail has been revived at the turn of the 21st century, and is currently enjoying a great surge in popularity. This explains why we are seeing a big revival of the cocktail hour, which takes place in the early evening, before dinner, and marks the transition from the busy working day to a time when relaxation and leisure take over in the evening.

Spirits
Spirits are at the heart of most cocktails. They provide both the original starting point for the concoction, as well as the powerful kick that lurks behind it.

The choice of different cocktails is enormous. There are a great many more cocktails than there are individual spirits, because each spirit can be mixed with any number of liqueurs, mixers, flavourings and decorations. The possible permutations are infinite.

♈ Gin is one of the most popular choices. It is a clear grain spirit further distilled with herb and fruit flavourings – the botanicals – that originated some 400 years ago in Holland, where it was originally used as a medicine. As it became increasingly available in cheap, adulterated forms, it moved further and further down the social scale until the 18th century when it was distilled from almost anything that would ferment and caused untold disease and distress. Nowadays there are many different excellent gins available. London dry gin is generally considered to be more suitable for making cocktails than the heavier Plymouth gin, or than the Dutch gins, which have a stronger flavour. Gin is the basic ingredient in that most famous of all cocktails, the Dry Martini.

♈ Vodka is virtually flavourless, which makes it a very good choice for cocktails as it adds a surprising depth to a concoction without actually affecting the flavour. This is what is known, in the trade, as being 'felt but not smelt'.

♈ Rum is distilled from sugar cane, with the West Indies and other parts of the Caribbean being the most common places of origin. Rum comes in both dark and white forms, with the dark rums being heavier in flavour than the pale types. Generally speaking, white rum is a particularly good choice in cocktails, while dark rum can be excellent in warming winter drinks such as hot punches – which are guaranteed to keep out the chill during even the coldest months of the year. Zombies are one of the most

potent rum cocktails, using both dark and light rums.

♈ Whisky is the oldest known spirit. Its origins are lost in the mists of time but there are official records dating from 15th century Scotland. Whisky also comes from Ireland (where it is spelled whiskey) and from the US (home of rye and Bourbon whiskey), though *aficionados* consider that Scotch is the only real whisky – as it has been made and drunk for generations in Scotland and it has played such an important role in the life of the Scottish nation. Of all the spirits, whisky is the one that is used the least in cocktails and, when it is used, it is usually only put in the more straightforward cocktails.

♈ Brandy means, literally 'burnt wine' in Dutch, and is distilled from fermented grape juice, or wine. The best-known examples

9

of brandy are made in France, notably Armagnac and Cognac.

Brandy can also be prepared from other fruits, such as apples (Calvados) and cherries (Kirsch). ⋎ Tequila is Mexico's national spirit. It is distilled from the sap of the blue agave plant, and is a relative newcomer in Europe, where it has only become popular since the 1960s. Since those early days, however, tequila has made up for lost time as two relatively recent cocktails – Tequila Sunrises and Margaritas – have become among the most popular cocktails that are drunk in modern cocktail bars.

Essential equipment

It is not really essential to have a lot of special equipment for cocktail making, and it is perfectly possible to make delicious cocktails with nothing more than a large jug and a spoon for mixing them. However, the paraphernalia involved in cocktail making has an irresistible glamour, and using some of the special equipment available, such as shakers and swizzle sticks, not only adds authenticity, it is also a lot of fun. The three basic pieces of cocktail equipment are a cocktail shaker, a mixing glass and a blender. The shaker is generally used for those drinks that require a really thorough shaking – these are often the ones that contain ingredients such as egg whites, syrups and fruit.

Shaken not stirred
Everyone remembers James Bond's immortal words, 'shaken, not

10

Sifter

Pourer

Shot glass

Salt saucer

Measures

Paring knife

Bar strainer

stirred', and this has become a sort of catch phrase. But what does it actually mean? Strictly speaking, clear drinks are usually stirred, while cloudy drinks, containing egg white, cream or fruit juices, are shaken. Shaken drinks can equally well be mixed in a blender. Shaken drinks are usually strained in order to remove anything that could spoil the appearance of the drink, such as pieces of ice and bits of fruit.

The cocktail shaker

It is perfectly possible to make cocktails without the aid of a cocktail shaker, but this helps, and if you are planning to make cocktails a regular part of your entertaining, it would not be a bad idea to invest in one. There are various different types of cocktail shaker, but the one you will usually come across consists of a deep container with a perforated screw-on top and an outer lid. The drink is added to the ice in the deep container, while both lids are screwed on. The outer lid is then removed, and the drink is poured through the perforations of the inner lid, which holds back the ice like a built-in strainer, and prevents the ice from splashing into the glass.

Never shake a fizzy drink, and do not fill a cocktail shaker more than four-fifths full. If you plan to serve a variety of different cocktails, it is a good idea to have (at least) two shakers, and to use one for drinks that contain highly flavoured ingredients, and the other for milder ones. This is advisable in order not to transfer

11

Straws

Cocktail shaker

Mixing glass

Blender

Cocktail sticks

Swizzle sticks

Parasols

Sugar syrup

Some cocktails and punches need to be sweetened, in which case the best way of doing this is probably to add a little sugar syrup, which will blend into a cold drink much more quickly than sugar. Sugar syrup is quick and easy to make, and it can be stored in a sterilized bottle in the refrigerator for up to two months.

To make sugar syrup, you will need:

4 tablespoons caster sugar
4 tablespoons of water

Put the sugar into a small saucepan with the water, and bring slowly to the boil, stirring continuously to dissolve the sugar. Then boil the mixture without stirring for 1–2 minutes.

strong, or wrong, flavours to drinks that would be spoiled by them.

It is also advisable to wash a shaker – or, for that matter, a mixing jug and stirrer – between using it for different cocktails. The reason for this is obviously the same – not transferring flavours to the wrong drinks.

The mixing glass

A mixing glass is used for those drinks that require only a gentle stirring before they are poured, or strained, into cocktail glasses. It should be large enough to make several servings of a cocktail at one time.

The blender

A blender is especially useful for making those drinks that contain fresh fruit, ice cream and milk. It is used, too, for making smoothies and milk shakes, or any other drinks of that sort.

Liqueur glass

Brandy balloon

Old-fashioned glass

Highball glass

Margarita glass

Additional essentials
In addition to those pieces of equipment, there are also other things that will come in useful for making cocktails. They are generally pieces of equipment that you will probably have around the kitchen already, so you will probably not need to buy many of these things specially. These are:

Ɏ a chopping board for cutting ingredients and decorations
Ɏ a sharp knife
Ɏ ice trays for freezing ice
Ɏ tongs to lift pieces of ice
Ɏ a long-handled spoon for mixing in the mixing glass
Ɏ a supply of cocktail sticks
Ɏ a corkscrew – it's actually a good idea to have more than one corkscrew to hand, as they are easy to mislay and a lost corkscrew could be disastrous!
Ɏ a supply of tea-towels

Ɏ a lemon squeezer
Ɏ an ice bucket

Not essential but nice to have around are:
Ɏ glass swizzle sticks
Ɏ coloured straws
Ɏ a set of bar measures for measuring quantities of drink

Glasses

You can use any number of different glasses for cocktails. There's absolutely nothing wrong with serving cocktails in ordinary wine glasses, or tumblers. Even the most fastidious connoisseur is actually highly unlikely to refuse a drink just because it's served in the 'wrong' glass. There aren't really any 'rules', other than a general one – the longer the drink, the taller the glass.

13

Wine glass

Hurricane glass

Pilsner glass

Champagne flute

Champagne flute

Classic cocktail glass

Cocktail glasses generally hold either 50 ml, 75 ml, 125 ml or 250 ml. There are, however, certain traditions, which you can follow or not, depending on your personal preference.

The classic cocktail glass has a V-shaped bowl set on a tall long stem.

An old-fashioned glass was originally designed for the classic cocktail of that name. It is a straight-sided tumbler, which holds 175–250 ml (6–8 fl oz). It is also a good glass for whisky, so you may already have a few of these glasses in your cupboard.

A highball glass was originally designed for this classic cocktail. It is a tall, straight-sided tumbler, which holds about 250 ml (8 fl oz). It is a particularly suitable glass to use for cocktails that are served over ice, such as Bloody Marys, and topped up with a mixer such as soda water or fruit juice.

A Margarita glass is a strange-shaped cocktail glass. It has a small bowl and a wide saucer shape on top, the rim of which is perfect for the salt that is traditionally used by Margarita drinkers.

Champagne flutes are a good choice for Champagne because their design prevents the bubbles from escaping from the glass, while the long stem prevents the drink being warmed by the drinker's hand. They are suitable for other fizzy drinks as well as Champagne or Champagne cocktails.

In addition, a couple of brandy balloons will also come in useful.

Making cocktails

Cocktails are surprisingly easy to make. If they are to be a success, however, there are certain golden rules to follow, which will guarantee that you get what you want every time in terms of both flavour and appearance.

Some of these rules may come as a surprise, while others will probably strike you as being very obvious. Either way, follow them, and you will quickly become the world's greatest expert in making cocktails.

℣ Keep all your ingredients in a cool place, particularly mixers and fruit juices, which should be chilled in the refrigerator.
℣ Always work, if you can, on a surface that will not be spoiled if drink is spilled or dripped on it, or if it is marked by glasses. It should be possible to wipe it easily.
℣ Similarly, keep a container of warm water at hand in order to rinse spoons or stirrers.
℣ Always serve iced drinks in chilled glasses.
℣ Similarly, serve hot punches and mulled wine in warmed glasses, the best being the ones that come with a metal holder.

The bartender's tips
The efficient bartender will run an efficient bar, the smooth running of which will be mostly due to careful foreplanning. Have all the ingredients you need ready to hand, and do as much as you can in advance. Have all your decorations prepared, so they are ready when you need them, and also make sure that you have

all the glasses, ice and whatever equipment you need ready.

The cocktail hour is a time for unwinding, not for getting into a last-minute panic, so think about what you need, make a list, and follow it. A successful cocktail party is one that runs smoothly, where the only hiccups you get are the ones you get as a result of drinking too many cocktails – and you won't get much sympathy for that!

Ice

Ice is one of the most important ingredients needed when making cocktails. Above all, don't try to skimp on ice – it's very important. In fact, you are almost bound to need much more ice than you think you will. Ice has two principal functions: one is obviously to chill the drink; the other is to act as a beater in the shaker.

If you're throwing a party, the ice can be made several days in advance and stored in the freezer until you need it. Tip the ice cubes into a large polythene bag and squirt them with soda water – this will keep the cubes separate from each other and stop them sticking together in the bag. Store the bag in the freezer or the freezing compartment of the refrigerator until required. Then store it in an ice bucket or a wine cooler, where you will be able to keep stockpiles of ice to hand ready for use when needed.

Ice cubes can also be obtained from specialist suppliers, and are sometimes available free of charge from the off-licence from which

15

you buy your alcoholic drinks, or from the fishmonger.

Some cocktails need cracked ice. To make this, put the cubes into a polythene bag, and hit it hard with a rolling pin or bang it against a wall until it is broken up.

Others use crushed ice – which cools a drink more, and faster than cracked ice. To make crushed ice,

put the cubes into a polythene bag as you did for cracked ice, and hammer hard using a rolling pin or hit it against the wall until it is finely broken up. Crushed ice needs to be more finely broken up than cracked ice.

For shaved ice, use a special shaver, which is not unlike a plane.

Make ice cubes in ice-making trays in a refrigerator or freezer. It is possible to find different trays for making specially shaped ice cubes – balls, wedges, squares, oblongs, hearts, even Christmas trees – and these can look effective in cocktails at a party.

The more ice you use in a cocktail, the cooler the drink will be. Remember, though, that too much ice will also dilute a drink. This is particularly true of crushed ice.

Decorative ice is a novel idea for party drinks. Fill a 'ball' ice tray with cocktail cherries, insert a cocktail stick if you wish, top up with water, and freeze. If you prefer, you can also set slices of lemon, lime or orange inside an ice cube, or why not try single raspberries? You can also use small sprigs of mint or lemon balm, all of which look very attractive in drinks.

Another idea is to use an edible food dye to colour ice-cubes. A few drops of yellow dye, a little lemon juice and thin slices of lemon cut to size, will make ice cubes look and taste wonderful. Similarly, you can use orange dye with orange slices, or green dye with lime slices, or red dye with cocktail cherries. Be imaginative, and see how many ideas you can come up with.

Decorating your cocktails

The decoration is very important; it is the crowning glory of any cocktail, and anyway, decorating cocktails is half the fun. Some cocktails demand that they be decorated in a certain way, as tradition dictates, and there is something almost ritualistic in these decorations. There has never been anything better, for decorating a Dry Martini, for example, than a green olive, plain or stuffed, or a twist of lemon rind. Similarly, a Manhattan cries out for a cocktail cherry.

With other cocktails, however, the choice is yours, and it's up to you and your imagination to come up with the most attractive decoration you can find. You can choose between the simple or the sumptuous, as the mood takes you. It's also important, though, to find something that's appropriate for that particular cocktail. An orange-flavoured cocktail, for example, would probably be best with an orange slice, while a few sprigs of fresh mint add both colour and flavour to a jug of Pimm's.

Try to select your decoration to relate to the cocktail in question but, other than this, the only

limit to your decorations is your imagination. Cocktails should be fun, and you can be as fancy or as outlandish as you like. Have a generous supply of cocktail sticks to hand, and decorate your drinks with olives, cocktail cherries, fresh fruit and sprigs of fresh herbs, or any combinations desired. Fresh fruit is often the perfect choice for decorating many cocktails and fruit punches. Strawberries make a particularly colourful and delicious decoration – spear them, whole or halved, with a cocktail stick. Similarly, raspberries, chunks of pineapple, wedges of melon, slices of mango or star fruit, pieces of banana or slices of cucumber will all add interest as well as flavour to your cocktails. Long spirals of orange, lemon and lime rind cut from the fruit in one piece take practice, but it's worth mastering the art because they look

so good – both attractive and professional. It's also a good idea to add any sprigs of fresh herbs,

such as mint, borage or lemon balm, according to which particular herb you think will lend the appropriate flavour.

Even bigger items such as celery leaves or sticks can look attractive, and can also be used to stir the cocktail. Wafers can be served with creamy cocktails.

There are also a number of things that you can sprinkle on top of the cocktail. Chocolate flakes, for example, can be used in chocolate-based drinks, while cocoa powder and coffee may also come in useful. Spices such as ground cinnamon, coriander and nutmeg can be effective for dusting cocktails and will look pretty as well as adding a special flavour.

Some drinks are traditionally decorated by decorating the glass itself, perhaps by coating the rim with sugar as for a Mint Julep, or with salt as for a Margarita,

to quote just two examples. To decorate the rim of the glass in this way, first run a slice of citrus fruit, such as lemon, lime or orange, around the rim of the glass in order to moisten it just a little. This is done to ensure that the salt stays firmly in place. Then dip the glass into a saucer of caster sugar or salt, as preferred or as required by the recipe, and tap gently to remove any excess.

Miniature cocktail parasols add colour to cocktails, and are useful for spearing olives and slices of lemon or lime. Swizzle sticks work well in fizzy drinks, and can be used to take some of the fizz out of a cocktail, while long drinks are often served with one or two coloured straws.

Broadly speaking, decorations can be divided into three basic categories. There are those that are served on the edge of the glass, such as a slice of citrus fruit; those that are speared on cocktail sticks, such as olives or cocktail cherries; and those that are floated in the drink, such as herb sprigs or spices. Whatever you decide to use, it is a very good idea to prepare your decorations in advance, so that they are ready when you need them.

Making citrus spirals

Citrus spirals are traditionally one of the most attractive decorations. You can use absolutely any citrus fruit that you like to make spirals – lemon, lime, orange or grapefruit. They can be long or short, as you prefer, and they look much more sophisticated than the ubiquitous slice. They add a professional touch and are actually surprisingly simple to make, with a bit of practice. Before you know it, you will have acquired a reputation as the slickest bartender in town!

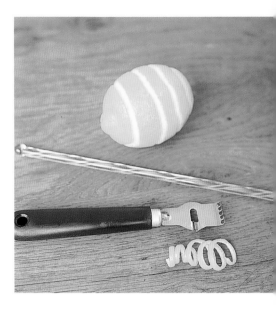

To make spirals, you really need to use a canelle knife that incorporates a parer, though failing this, a swivel-headed vegetable or potato peeler can be used instead, or even a small sharp knife.

To make a spiral, follow this procedure.

1 Hold the citrus fruit in one hand and the implement in the other.

2 Starting at one end, carve around the fruit slowly and carefully. Include a little pith along with the rind to give it some body, but do not include too much.

3 When you have removed a long strip from the fruit, wind it tightly around a drinking straw or, even better, around a glass swizzle stick, to curl it into a spiral. An alternative to this is to wind the rind around something slightly thicker, such as the handle of a wooden spoon. This will produce a larger, looser spiral, which would be particularly suitable for decorating something bigger such as a punch bowl or a big jug containing the colourful cocktail of your choice.

4 When your spirals are ready, add them to the cocktails. By far the

easiest way of doing this is just to drape them over the side of the glass. Alternatively, they can be tied into bows or knots, speared on a cocktail stick and then arranged over the edges of each glass, perhaps – if you like – with an olive or a cocktail cherry, though this is a rather more complicated way of doing things and is strictly optional. Other things you can try as you become more familiar with your role behind the bar, as it were, are to frame a cherry with a spiral, or to make an arrangement on a cocktail stick with a cherry flanked by spirals wound into the shape of your choice. Experiment with decorations – you will be surprised by the range of possibilities as you become more practised.

Throwing a cocktail party

A cocktail party is a very convivial occasion, at which cocktails are likely to be the only drinks on offer. It is also a relatively simple way of entertaining a few friends without going to all the trouble of preparing a meal. It's a festive occasion, perfect for celebrating a special event – an engagement, perhaps, or a birthday for a special person, a business success, a welcome to new neighbours, or a thank-you for old and valued friends. Either way and whatever the reason, a cocktail party is usually bound to fit the bill.

Cocktail parties were especially popular in upper-class society in the 1920s and '30s, so it would be fun to ask your guests if they would like to dress up in '20s and '30s costumes. If they're not sure what to wear, ask the men to wear tails or a smart casual jacket with grey flannel trousers, and ask the women to wear pretty, ankle-length chiffon dresses. You'll be

amazed by how much effort they put into the occasion, when they turn up looking like extras for parts in *The Great Gatsby*. Cocktails will, of course, be the only drinks that you will have to serve at this sort of party. So plan the drinks, freeze the ice, and get shaking ...

Most people like cocktails, whether drinking one or two as an aperitif before a meal, or indulging in rather more at a full-scale cocktail party. They are therefore a good way of entertaining friends. The cocktail hour is usually between 6 and 8 pm, and doesn't usually run for more than two hours.

Don't forget, in your enthusiasm, to cater for those who won't be drinking alcohol – perhaps because they prefer not to, or because they will be driving home. Always offer a choice of non-alcoholic drinks, such as mineral water and fruit juices, or – as this is a cocktail party, after all – a delicious fruit cocktail or punch.

To plan the drinks for your party you must, first of all, decide which, and how many, cocktails you're going to offer. About three is usually a good number – perhaps a wine-based cocktail such as a Kir Royale or Buck's Fizz; one based on fruit juice such as a Screwdriver or a Piña Colada, and some sort of spirit-based cocktail such as a Dry Martini or a White Russian.

As cocktail parties are usually held early in the evening, it is usually assumed that the guests will go out to dinner later. This means you won't need to serve very much in the way of food at a cocktail party but a few canapés and sim-

ple bite-sized nibbles will add to the atmosphere and will also help soak up some of the alcohol and prevent people drinking too much. Reckon on about six to eight items of food per person, and offer a selection of three or four different items. Don't choose anything fussy or messy and, if you're short of time and can't prepare snacks and nibbles specially for your guests, just scatter a few bowls around the room, with a simple selection of bought nibbles, such as olives, nuts and raisins. Cold food is much easier to provide than hot food. Dips with savoury crackers or crudités are another good choice. Always provide lots of paper napkins to clean fingers and wipe up spills, and have plenty of cocktail sticks on hand for people to use with any items of food that are particularly greasy or sticky.

23

Estimating quantities

It is difficult to estimate quantities
when you're making your shop-
ping list, and this will obviously
require some careful thought.
In the event, guests may surprise
you by drinking much less –
or usually much more! – than
you had expected. As a rough
guide, the following may act as
a rough and ready guide. Allow
30 single measures per bottle
for spirits and vermouths. You
will get between 16 and 20
drinks when you are adding a
mixer to these, such as soda
water, tonic water, fruit juice,
or whatever else is desired.

The average size of wine
bottle will give you between five
to six glasses, while Champagne

will usually give you six to eight glasses. A 600 ml (1 pint) carton of fruit juice should yield seven to ten drinks.

You should probably reckon on serving about three or four drinks per person – perhaps as many as five for heavy drinkers.

The Classics

There are a great many cocktails that, for most people, seem to encapsulate everything that the perfect cocktail should be: style, sophistication and flavour. These are the traditional favourites, from the perfect Dry Martini to the Harvey Wallbanger, or from the Whiskey Sour to the definitive Bloody Mary. They are probably the most powerful expression of the late twentieth-century revival of the cocktail. This chapter contains recipes for some of the best all-time greats. They'll ring a bell, they'll tweak the taste-buds, and they'll pack a punch!

Reputedly named after its creator, a New York barman named Martini, the earliest Dry Martinis, before 1914, may have contained equal proportions of gin and dry vermouth. Since then, the drink seems to have become drier and drier, so that nowadays proportions of 15:1 (just a dash of dry vermouth) are not unknown, although the most common is 4:1.

Dry Martini

Put the ice cubes into a mixing glass. Pour the vermouth and gin over the ice and stir (never shake) vigorously and evenly without splashing, then strain into a chilled cocktail glass. Serve with a green olive and a strip of lemon rind.

5–6 ice cubes
½ measure dry vermouth
3 measures gin
1 green olive and a thin strip of lemon rind, to decorate

🕐 Preparation time: 2 minutes
🍸 Serves 1

'Shaken, not stirred' these words were immortalized by James Bond in his Martini instructions.

28

Gin Sling

Put the ice cubes into a cocktail shaker. Pour the lemon juice, cherry brandy and gin over the ice and shake until a frost forms. Pour, without straining, into a hurricane glass and top up with soda water. Decorate with cherries, if liked, and serve with 1–2 straws.

4–5 ice cubes
juice of ½ lemon
1 measure cherry brandy
3 measures gin
soda water
cherries, to decorate (optional)

🕐 Preparation time: 3 minutes
🍸 Serves 1

Cherry brandy
Cherry brandy is a liqueur that is made by macerating cherries in brandy, not by distilling brandy from cherries.

Mint
The sprigs of a great many different varieties of mint, such as spearmint and applemint, can all be used in cocktails. Their bright green leaves are both refreshing and attractive.

Mint Julep

Crush the mint with the caster sugar in an old-fashioned glass or large tumbler and rub it around the inside of the glass. Discard the mint. Dissolve the sugar in the soda water, add the ice and pour over the Bourbon. Do not stir. Decorate with the sprig of mint.

3 sprigs of mint

½ teaspoon caster sugar

1 tablespoon soda water

2–3 ice cubes, crushed

1 measure Bourbon whiskey

sprig of mint, to decorate

🕐 Preparation time: 3 minutes

🍸 Serves 1

Manhattan

Put the ice cubes into a mixing glass. Pour the
vermouth and whiskey over the ice. Stir vigorously,
then strain into a chilled cocktail glass. To serve,
add a cherry, if liked.

4–5 ice cubes
1 measure sweet vermouth
3 measures rye or bourbon whiskey
1 cocktail cherry, to
        decorate (optional)

🕐 Preparation time: 2 minutes

🍸 Serves 1

'A narrow island off the
coast of New Jersey devoted to the
pursuit of lunch' was how journalist
Raymond Sokolov described this
famous area of New York.

*One of the Alexander family, this cocktail is the younger –
but no less powerful – brother of the classic gin and
brandy cocktails, the Alexander and the Brandy Alexander.*

Alexander Baby *right*

Put the ice cubes into a cocktail shaker and pour the
rum, crème de cacao and cream over the ice. Shake
until a frost forms, then strain into a chilled cocktail
glass. Sprinkle grated nutmeg on top.

4–5 ice cubes
2 measures dark rum
1 measure crème de cacao
½ measure double cream
grated nutmeg, to decorate

🕐 Preparation time: 3 minutes
🍸 Serves 1

*'There's nought, no doubt, so
much the spirit calms / As rum and true
religion', suggested Lord Byron in his epic
satire Don Juan.*

Cuba Libre

Place the ice cubes in a tall tumbler and pour the
rum and lime juice over them. Stir to mix. Top up
with cola, decorate with a slice of lime and drink
with a straw.

2–3 ice cubes
1½ measures dark rum
juice of ½ lime
cola, to top up
slice of lime, to decorate

🕐 Preparation time: 2 minutes
🍸 Serves 1

Cuban rum
Cuba has always been known for its light, rather than dark,
rum. Bacardi was made famous by the novelist Ernest
Hemingway. It is no longer produced in Cuba, but in Nassau
in the Bahamas.

The Daiquiri was invented by an American mining engineer working in Cuba in 1896. He was expecting some high-powered guests, but his supplies of gin had run out, so he experimented with rum – and one of the world's favourite cocktails was born.

Daiquiri *right*

Put lots of cracked ice into a cocktail shaker. Pour the lime juice, sugar syrup and rum over the ice. Shake thoroughly until a frost forms, then strain into a chilled cocktail glass.

cracked ice
juice of 2 limes
1 teaspoon sugar syrup (see page 12)
3 measures white rum

🕐 Preparation time: 3 minutes
🍸 Serves 1

You do not have to be lying on a palm-lined, golden beach, staring at an endless expanse of deep blue sea, with the hot Caribbean sun beating down to quench your thirst with this tropical concoction – just one sip and you will think you are.

34

Piña Colada

Place the cracked ice, rum, coconut cream and pineapple juice in a cocktail shaker. Shake lightly to mix. Strain into a large glass and decorate with the cherry and orange slice.

cracked ice
1 measure white rum
2 measures coconut cream
2 measures pineapple juice
To Decorate:
1 cocktail cherry
slice of orange

🕐 Preparation time: 3 minutes
🍸 Serves 1

'Bring me two piña colada / One for each hand / Let's set sail with Captain Morgan / Though we'll never leave dry land.' Singer Garth Brooks knew a thing or two about how to forget his troubles and dream of being somewhere better.

Brandy Classic

Put the ice cubes into a cocktail shaker. Pour in the brandy, Curaçao, maraschino liqueur and lemon juice and shake together. Strain into a chilled cocktail glass. Add some cracked ice and a wedge of lemon and serve.

🕐 Preparation time: 3 minutes

🍸 Serves 1

4–5 ice cubes
1 measure brandy
1 measure blue Curaçao
1 measure maraschino liqueur
juice of ½ lemon
cracked ice
lemon wedge, to decorate

Blue Curaçao
A dazzling blue, orange-flavoured liqueur, made with the dried peel of the green oranges that come from the Caribbean island of the same name. It is also available in several other colours.

Nog was originally a strong beer brewed in East Anglia in eastern England, so perhaps the original egg nog was a mixture of egg, milk and beer – a nourishing, but unpalatable combination. A noggin, however, was a liquid measure equivalent to 150 ml/¼ pint, so maybe the drink has always been based on brandy and a noggin of milk.

Egg Nog

Half fill a cocktail shaker with ice. Add the egg, sugar syrup, brandy and milk and shake well for about 1 minute. Strain into a tumbler and sprinkle with a little grated nutmeg. Drink with a straw, if liked.

🕐 Preparation time: 2 minutes
🍸 Serves 1

4–5 ice cubes
1 egg
1 tablespoon sugar syrup (see page 12)
2 measures brandy
150 ml (¼ pint) milk
grated nutmeg, to decorate

'He who aspires to be a hero ... must drink brandy', affirmed Dr Samuel Johnson, according to his biographer.

37

Brandy Sour *left*

Put the ice cubes into a cocktail shaker. Shake the bitters over the ice, add the lemon juice, brandy and sugar syrup and shake until a frost forms. Strain into a tumbler and decorate with lemon slices on a cocktail stick. Serve with a straw.

🕐 Preparation time: 3 minutes
🍸 Serves 1

4–5 ice cubes
3 drops Angostura bitters
juice of 1 lemon
3 measures brandy
1 teaspoon sugar syrup (see page 12)
slices of lemon, to decorate

Whiskey Sour
An equally classic cocktail is made with the same quantity of Bourbon whiskey instead of brandy.

Between the Sheets *below*

Put the ice cubes into a cocktail shaker. Add the brandy, white rum, Cointreau, lemon juice and sugar syrup and shake until a frost forms. Strain into a chilled cocktail glass.

🕐 Preparation time: 3 minutes
🍸 Serves 1

4–5 ice cubes
1¼ measures brandy
1 measure white rum
½ measure Cointreau
¾ measure fresh lemon juice
½ measure sugar syrup (see page 12)

Brandy Alexander

Put the ice into a cocktail shaker and add the brandy, crème de cacao and cream. Shake well to mix thoroughly and strain into a cocktail glass. Sprinkle with grated nutmeg.

2–3 ice cubes, cracked
1 measure brandy
1 measure crème de cacao
1 measure double cream
grated nutmeg, to decorate

🕐 Preparation time: 3 minutes

🍸 Serves 1

'Cocoa? Cocoa? Damn miserable puny stuff, fit for kittens and unwashed boys.' Shirley Jackson had clearly never tried a Brandy Alexander.

Luigi

Put the ice cubes into a mixing glass. Pour the
orange juice, vermouth, Cointreau, grenadine
and gin over the ice and stir vigorously. Strain
into a chilled cocktail glass, decorate with the
orange slice and serve.

🕐 Preparation time: 2 minutes
🍸 Serves 1

4–5 ice cubes
1 measure fresh orange juice
1 measure dry vermouth
½ measure Cointreau
1 measure grenadine
2 measures gin
slice of orange, to decorate

Grenadine
An extremely sweet, bright pink, non-alcoholic
pomegranate syrup from France.

This is one of many cocktails that has altered with changing tastes since it was invented in the 1930s, when it was based on gin, rather than vodka, and mixed with grenadine and lemon juice instead of cranberry and grapefruit juice.

Sea Breeze *right*

Pour the vodka, cranberry juice and grapefruit juice into a hurricane or tall glass with the ice cubes and stir to mix well. Decorate with a wedge of lemon or lime and drink with a straw.

1 measure vodka
1½ measures cranberry juice
1½ measures fresh grapefruit juice
5 ice cubes, crushed
lemon or lime wedge, to decorate

🕐 Preparation time: 2 minutes
🍸 Serves 1

Cranberry juice
This scarlet berry is known for its good bouncing properties. People used to tip them down the steps to test their quality – the good ones kept on bouncing, while the bad ones stayed where they first fell.

42

French Leave

Put the ice cubes in a cocktail shaker and add the vodka, orange juice and Pernod. Shake until a frost forms, then strain into a cocktail glass.

2–3 ice cubes
2 measures vodka
1 measure fresh orange juice
1 measure Pernod

🕐 Preparation time: 3 minutes
🍸 Serves 1

Pernod
This is probably the best-known type of pastis. Flavoured with aniseed, it is usually drunk in France as an aperitif, when it is mixed with water which turns it cloudy.

Invented in the 1960s, this is said to be named after a Californian surfer called Harvey. He developed such a taste for Screwdrivers topped with Galliano and drank so many of them that, on leaving the bar, he would bounce off the walls.

Harvey Wallbanger *left*

Put half of the ice cubes, the vodka and orange juice into a cocktail shaker. Shake well for about 30 seconds, then strain into a tall glass over the remaining ice cubes. Float the Galliano on top and decorate with orange slices.

6 ice cubes
1 measure vodka
125 ml (4 fl oz) fresh orange juice
1–2 teaspoons Galliano
slices of orange, to decorate

● Preparation time: 2 minutes
Ŧ Serves 1

Galliano
Galliano is a pale amber liqueur from Italy, tasting strongly of herbs. It has been available since 1960 and is sold in distinctive fluted bottles.

45

The delicious and refreshing simplicity of the Screwdriver has inspired a number of other cocktails, notably the Harvey Wallbanger and the Sloe Comfortable Screw.

Screwdriver

Put the ice cubes into a tall glass. Add the vodka and orange juice and stir lightly.

2–3 ice cubes
1 measure vodka
2 measures fresh orange juice or
   juice of 1 orange

● Preparation time: 2 minutes
Ŧ Serves 1

The best and most famous Bloody Mary ever was created in Harry's Bar in New York.

Bloody Mary *right*

Put all the ingredients into a cocktail shaker and shake, then strain into a tall glass or wine glass. Add your chosen decoration.

🕐 Preparation time: 3 minutes
🍸 Serves 1

1 measure vodka
3 measures tomato juice
2 dashes Worcestershire sauce
good squeeze of lemon juice
dash of Tabasco sauce
3 ice cubes
salt and pepper, to taste
slice of lemon, sprig of mint
    or stick of celery, to decorate

Long Island Iced Tea

Put the ice cubes into a mixing glass. Add the gin, vodka, rum, tequila, Cointreau, lemon juice and sugar syrup. Stir well, then strain into a tall glass almost filled with ice cubes. Top up with cola and decorate with the slice of lemon.

🕐 Preparation time: 3 minutes
🍸 Serves 1

6 ice cubes
½ measure gin
½ measure vodka
½ measure white rum
½ measure tequila
½ measure Cointreau
1 measure fresh lemon juice
½ teaspoon sugar syrup (see
    page 12)
cola, to top up
slice of lemon, to decorate

Sex on the Beach

Put the vodka, peach schnapps, cranberry juice, orange juice and pineapple juice, if using, into a cocktail shaker with the ice. Shake thoroughly. Pour into a tall glass, decorate with the cherry and drink with a straw.

🕐 Preparation time: 3 minutes
🍸 Serves 1

½ measure vodka
½ measure peach schnapps
1 measure cranberry juice
1 measure fresh orange juice
1 measure pineapple juice
    (optional)
3 ice cubes
1 cocktail cherry, to decorate

Traditionally, tequila is served in a shot glass with salt and a wedge of lime. The salt is sprinkled on the back of the hand between the thumb and forefinger, which grasp the lime. On downing the tequila, the drinker immediately licks the salt and sucks the lime. This somewhat inelegant performance gave rise to one of today's most popular cocktails.

Margarita *left*

Put the tequila, lime juice and Cointreau into a cocktail shaker with the cracked ice. Shake thoroughly and strain into a cocktail glass rimmed with salt, if using. Decorate with a slice of lime.

1½ measures tequila
1 measure fresh lime juice
1 measure Cointreau
2–3 ice cubes, cracked
salt, for rimming (optional)
slice of lime, to decorate

Preparation time: 3 minutes
Serves 1

'Wasting away in Margaritaville / Searching for my lost shaker of salt' – there are worse ways of getting over a broken heart than Jimmy Buffet's.

49

Tequila Sunrise

Crack half of the ice and put it in a cocktail shaker. Add the tequila and orange juice and shake to mix. Put the remaining ice into a tall glass and strain the tequila over it. Slowly pour in the grenadine and allow to settle. Stir once before serving.

5–6 ice cubes
1 measure tequila
2½ measures fresh orange juice
2 teaspoons grenadine

Preparation time: 3 minutes
Serves 1

Tequila Cocktail

Put the ice cubes in a cocktail shaker. Add the tequila, port, lime juice and Angostura bitters and shake well. Strain into a cocktail glass and decorate with a slice of lime.

2–3 ice cubes, cracked
1 measure tequila
½ measure port
1 teaspoon fresh lime juice
2 dashes Angostura bitters
slice of lime, to decorate

Preparation time: 3 minutes
Serves 1

Classic Champagne Cocktail *right*

Put the sugar lump into a chilled cocktail or champagne glass and saturate with the bitters. Add the brandy, then fill the glass with Champagne. Decorate with the slice of orange.

1 sugar lump
1–2 dashes Angostura bitters
1 measure brandy
4 measures chilled Champagne
slice of orange, to decorate

🕐 Preparation time: 2 minutes
🍸 Serves 1

'...full of beauty after drinking it' was how Madame de Pompadour, mistress of Louis XV of France, was described when she had been quaffing Champagne.*

Angostura bitters
This strangely medicinal concoction was developed by a German doctor in the South American town of Angostura in the nineteenth century. It was originally intended for medicinal use and was taken in gin by the Royal Navy; this is how Pink Gin came about.

Traditionally, Bollinger Champagne is used,. but it still tastes good with other brands.

Buck's Fizz

Put the orange juice and grenadine in a wine glass or champagne flute and stir well. Top up with chilled Champagne.

1 measure chilled fresh orange juice
1 dash of grenadine
2 measures chilled Champagne

🕐 Preparation time: 2 minutes
🍸 Serves 1

B-52

Pour the Kahlúa into a liqueur or shot glass. Using
the back of a spoon, slowly pour the Bailey's to
float over the Kahlúa. Pour the Grand Marnier over
the Bailey's in the same way. This will result in a
three-layered shooter.

½ **measure Kahlúa**
½ **measure Bailey's Irish Cream**
½ **measure Grand Marnier**

🕐 Preparation time: 4 minutes
🍸 Serves 1

Kahlúa
**Kahlúa is a coffee-flavoured liqueur which comes
from Mexico.**

Grasshopper

Pour the crème de cacao into a glass. Pour the
crème de menthe gently over the back of a
teaspoon so that it floats on top and serve.

1 measure crème de cacao
1 measure crème de menthe

🕐 Preparation time: 3 minutes
🍸 Serves 1

Crème de cacao
This is a sweet liqueur, made from cocoa beans and
vanilla. Use sparingly in a cocktail, as the ultra sweet
flavour of chocolate is highly potent.

Strictly Spirits

The great majority of the best cocktails are based on spirits, and there are many of these that can be used as the starting point for delicious concoctions for sipping in convivial company. Gin, vodka, rum, brandy and whisky; whatever ranks at the top of your list of favourite spirits, it can be put to good use in a delicious cocktail. Whether you're looking for a long, languorous drink, such as a Salty Dog, a powerful concoction that packs a truly treacherous kick like a Knockout, or an interesting combination of flavours like a Stormy Weather, we have the perfect recipe for you.

Burnsides

Put 4–5 ice cubes into a cocktail shaker. Dash the bitters over the ice, add the cherry brandy, sweet and dry vermouths and gin. Shake lightly, then strain into a glass over the remaining ice cubes. Decorate with strips of lemon rind.

8–10 ice cubes
2 drops Angostura bitters
1 teaspoon cherry brandy
1 measure sweet vermouth
2 measures dry vermouth
2 measures gin
strips of lemon rind,
to decorate

🕐 Preparation time: 3 minutes

🍸 Serves 1

'I am willing to taste any drink once'. James Branch Cabell's words are a good motto for anyone experimenting with cocktails.

The sharp flavours of this cocktail are enough to make anyone's scalp tingle. For a really mouth-puckering version, substitute dry for the sweet vermouth.

Hair Raiser

Put the ice cubes into a tall glass and pour the vodka, vermouth and tonic over them. Stir lightly. Decorate with the spirals of lemon and lime and drink with a straw.

🕐 Preparation time: 2 minutes
🍸 Serves 1

1–2 ice cubes, cracked
1 measure vodka
1 measure sweet vermouth
1 measure tonic water
lemon and lime rind spirals,
    to decorate

'I could a tale unfold …

would make … each particular hair to stand on end …'

A racer of a cocktail that should really start your heart pounding – without flagging. However, it's best to be a back seat driver on the way home after the party.

Le Mans

Put the ice into a tall glass. Add the Cointreau and vodka, stir and top up with soda. Float the slice of lemon on top.

🕐 Preparation time: 2 minutes
🍸 Serves 1

2–3 cracked ice cubes
1 measure Cointreau
½ measure vodka
soda water, to top up
slice of lemon, to decorate

Wrinklies Rule

Put the ice cubes into a tall glass. Add the vodka, Campari and orange juice and stir well. Top up with soda water and float the orange slice on top.

🕐 Preparation time: 2 minutes
🍸 Serves: 1

2–3 cracked ice cubes
2 measures vodka
1 measure Campari
½ measure fresh orange juice
soda water, to top up
slice of lemon, to decorate

Although traditionally, a gin-based cocktail, Salty Dog can also be made with vodka instead. The rim of the glass can be frosted with salt, like a Margarita, for extra sparkle.

Salty Dog

Put the ice cubes into an old-fashioned glass. Put the salt on the ice and add the gin and grapefruit juice. Stir gently, decorate with a slice of orange and serve.

🕐 Preparation time: 3 minutes

🍸 Serves 1

2–3 ice cubes

pinch of salt

1 measure gin

2–2½ measures fresh
    grapefruit juice

slice of orange,
    to decorate

This refreshing cooler is a gin-based variation of the classic bourbon whiskey cocktail, Mint Julep.

Gin Cup

Put the mint and sugar syrup into an old-fashioned glass and stir them about to bruise the mint slightly. Fill the glass with chopped ice, add the lemon juice and gin and stir until a frost begins to form. Decorate with extra mint sprigs.

🕐 Preparation time: 3 minutes
🍸 Serves 1

3 sprigs of mint, plus extra
 to decorate
1 teaspoon sugar syrup (see
 page 12)
chopped ice
juice of ½ lemon
3 measures gin

*At least part of the pleasure of this pale coloured cocktail is
the surprise of the minty flavour when you first taste it. You
can also make it with green crème de menthe and sweet
white vermouth, in which case it becomes a One Two.*

Knockout

Put the ice cubes into a mixing glass. Pour the
vermouth, crème de menthe and gin over the
ice, stir vigorously, then strain into a chilled old-
fashioned glass. Add the Pernod and decorate
with a slice of lemon.

4–5 ice cubes

1 measure dry vermouth

½ measure white crème
   de menthe

2 measures gin

1 drop of Pernod

slice of lemon, to decorate

🕐 Preparation time: 3 minutes

🍸 Serves 1

This popular cocktail has spawned a number of variations, such as the Pink Clover Club, in which grenadine is substituted for the sugar syrup, creating a pretty pink drink. It can be further enhanced by decorating it with a strawberry or cocktail cherries speared on a cocktail stick.

Clover Club

Put the ice cubes into a cocktail shaker. Pour the lime juice, sugar syrup, egg white and gin over the ice and shake until a frost forms. Strain into a tumbler and serve decorated with grated lime rind and a lime wedge.

🕐 Preparation time: 3 minutes

🍸 Serves 1

4–5 ice cubes

juice of 1 lime

½ teaspoon sugar syrup (see
    page 12)

1 egg white

3 measures gin

To Decorate:

grated lime rind

lime wedge

61

Opera

Put the ice cubes into a mixing glass. Pour the Dubonnet, Curaçao and gin over the ice. Stir evenly, then strain into a chilled cocktail glass. Decorate with the orange rind spiral and serve.

🕐 Preparation time: 3 minutes

🍸 Serves 1

4–5 ice cubes
1 measure Dubonnet
½ measure Curaçao
2 measures gin
orange rind spiral, to decorate

Dubonnet
This is a red wine-based aperitif, flavoured with the essence of a tropical tree bark and quinine. A white version is also available.

Chocolate and orange make a classic combination, so crème de cacao and Cointreau form a sensational partnership to flavour this gin-based cocktail.

Crossbow

Put the ice cubes into a cocktail shaker and add the gin, crème de cacao and Cointreau. Dampen the rim of a chilled cocktail glass with a little water then dip the rim into a saucer of drinking chocolate. Shake the cocktail shaker vigorously, then strain the drink into the glass.

4–5 ice cubes
½ measure gin
½ measure crème de cacao
½ measure Cointreau
drinking chocolate powder, to decorate

● Preparation time: 3 minutes

🍸 Serves 1

Whisky Sour was the original classic cocktail, but the mixture works just as well with vodka. It can also be made into a longer drink by pouring it into a highball glass after shaking and then topping up with soda water and omitting the bitters. Sometimes lime juice is substituted for the lemon.

Vodka Sour

Put the ice cubes into a cocktail shaker, add the vodka, sugar syrup, egg white and lemon juice and shake until a frost forms. Pour without straining into a cocktail glass and shake 3 drops of Angostura bitters on the top to decorate.

🕐 Preparation time: 3 minutes

🍸 Serves 1

4–5 ice cubes

2 measures vodka

½ measure sugar syrup (see page 12)

1 egg white

1½ measures fresh lemon juice

3 drops Angostura bitters, to decorate

Stormy Weather

Put the ice cubes into a cocktail shaker and add the gin, Mandarine Napoléon and dry and sweet vermouths. Shake to mix and strain into a chilled cocktail glass. Decorate the rim of the glass with the spiral of orange.

🕐 Preparation time: 3 minutes

🍸 Serves 1

3 ice cubes, cracked

1½ measures gin

¼ Mandarine Napoléon liqueur

¼ measure dry vermouth

¼ measure sweet vermouth

orange rind spiral, to decorate

This ever-popular, classic cocktail has inspired a number of others. For a Pink Lady, substitute grenadine for the Cointreau and omit the lemon juice. For a Fair Lady, substitute grapefruit juice for the lemon juice.

White Lady *right*

Place the gin, Cointreau, lemon juice and egg white in a cocktail shaker. Shake to mix, then strain into a cocktail glass. Decorate with the spiral of lemon.

2 measures gin

1 measure Cointreau

1 teaspoon fresh lemon juice

about ½ teaspoon egg white

lemon rind spiral, to decorate

🕐 Preparation time: 3 minutes

🍸 Serves 1

This was traditionally made with Plymouth gin, which has a stronger flavour of herbs than London gin – the usual base for cocktails. Connoisseurs say that it is simply not the same if made with anything other than Plymouth gin.

Pink Gin

Shake the bitters into a cocktail glass and roll them around until the sides are well coated. Add the gin, then top up with iced water, to taste.

1–4 dashes Angostura bitters

1 measure gin

iced water, to top up

🕐 Preparation time: 3 minutes

🍸 Serves 1

Gimlet

Put the ice into an old-fashioned glass, pour the lime cordial over the ice and stir. Add the gin, stir and decorate with a slice of lime.

4–5 ice cubes

1 measure lime cordial

2 measures gin

slice of lime, to decorate

🕐 Preparation time: 2 minutes

🍸 Serves 1

'A real gimlet is half gin and half Rose's lime juice and nothing else. It beats martinis hollow.' Raymond Chandler's famous private eye, Philip Marlowe, is introduced to the cocktail in The Long Good-bye.

A milk punch is traditionally made with Scotch whisky, but you could use Irish whiskey or even bourbon for a change, if you prefer their flavours.

Whisky Milk Punch *left*

Put the ice cubes into a cocktail shaker. Pour the sugar syrup, whisky and milk over the ice and shake until a frost forms. Pour, without straining, into an old-fashioned glass, sprinkle with grated nutmeg and serve.

4–5 ice cubes
1 teaspoon sugar syrup (see page 12)
2 measures whisky
3 measures milk
grated nutmeg

🕐 Preparation time: 3 minutes
🍸 Serves 1

'Freedom and Whisky gang *together', according to Robert Burns.*

Golden Daisy

Put the ice cubes into a cocktail shaker. Pour the lemon juice, sugar syrup, Cointreau and whisky over the ice and shake vigorously until a frost forms. Strain into an old-fashioned glass and serve decorated with a lime wedge.

4–5 ice cubes
juice of 1 lemon
1 teaspoon sugar syrup (see page 12)
½ measure Cointreau
3 measures whisky
lime wedge, to decorate

🕐 Preparation time: 3 minutes
🍸 Serves 1

Roamin' the Gloamin'

Put the ice cubes in a cocktail shaker. Add the whisky, Cointreau and orange juice and shake until a frost forms. Pour into a old-fashioned glass and decorate with a slice of orange.

4–5 ice cubes
2 measures Scotch whisky
1 measure Cointreau
2 tablespoons fresh orange juice
slice of orange, to decorate

🕐 Preparation time: 3 minutes
🍸 Serves 1

Southerly Buster *right*

Put the ice cubes into a mixing glass. Pour the
Curaçao and whisky over the ice, stir vigorously,
then strain into a chilled cocktail glass. Twist the
lemon rind over the drink and drop it in. Serve
with a straw.

4–5 ice cubes
1 measure blue Curaçao
3 measures whisky
lemon rind, to decorate

🕐 Preparation time: 3 minutes
🍸 Serves 1

*The name of this cocktail perfectly describes its
beautiful golden colour, but is no reflection of its flavour.*

Rusty Nail

Put the ice into a small tumbler and pour over
the whisky. Pour the Drambuie over the back of
a teaspoon on top of the whisky. Decorate the
rim of the glass with a spiral of lemon.

2–3 ice cubes
1 measure Scotch whisky
½ measure Drambuie
lemon rind spiral, to decorate

🕐 Preparation time: 3 minutes
🍸 Serves 1

70

Drambuie
**This is a Scotch whisky liqueur flavoured with heather
honey and herbs. It is said to be made according a recipe
from Bonnie Prince Charlie.**

Ross and Cromarty

Put the ice cubes in a cocktail shaker. Pour the
whisky, Kahlúa and cream over the ice and shake
until a frost forms. Strain into a cocktail glass and
sprinkle with a pinch of nutmeg.

4–5 ice cubes
1 measure whisky
1 measure Kahlúa
3 tablespoons single cream
grated nutmeg, to decorate

🕐 Preparation time: 3 minutes
🍸 Serves 1

Tar *left*

Put the ice cubes into a cocktail shaker. Pour in the lemon juice, grenadine, crème de cacao and whisky. Shake until a frost forms, then strain into a chilled cocktail glass. Serve with a straw.

🕐 Preparation time: 3 minutes

🍸 Serves 1

4–5 ice cubes

juice of 1 lemon

½ teaspoon grenadine

1 measure crème de cacao

3 measures whisky

'Alcohol is a liquid that can put the wreck into recreation', ruefully reflected an anonymous imbiber.

Bobby Burns

Put the ice into a cocktail shaker and add the whisky, vermouth and Bénédictine. Shake until a frost forms, then strain into a chilled cocktail glass and decorate with a strip of lemon rind.

🕐 Preparation time: 3 minutes

🍸 Serves 1

4–5 ice cubes

1 measure Scotch whisky

1 measure dry vermouth

1 tablespoon Bénédictine

strip of lemon rind,
    to decorate

73

'John Barleycorn should die.' Scotch was clearly as close to Robert Burns' heart as Scotland.

Bénédictine
This world-famous liqueur has been produced by Bénédictine monks since the early sixteenth century. It is flavoured with aromatic herbs and spices according to a secret recipe.

Algonquin

Put the ice cubes into a mixing glass. Pour the pineapple juice, vermouth and whisky over the ice. Stir vigorously, until nearly frothy, then strain into a chilled cocktail glass. Serve decorated with a cocktail parasol and drink with a straw.

Preparation time: 3 minutes
Serves 1

4–5 ice cubes
1 measure unsweetened pineapple juice
1 measure dry vermouth
3 measures bourbon or Scotch whisky

Skipper

Put the ice cubes into a mixing glass. Pour the
grenadine over the ice and add the orange juice,
vermouth and whisky. Stir vigorously, until nearly
frothy, then pour into a tumbler. Decorate with an
orange slice and serve with a straw.

🕐 Preparation time: 3 minutes

🍸 Serves 1

4–5 ice cubes
4 drops grenadine
juice of ½ orange
1 measure dry vermouth
3 measures rye or
    Scotch whisky
orange wedge, to decorate

This is a younger member of the Collins family of cocktails, of which John or, sometimes, Tom – a gin-based drink – was the first. There are others, too. Pierre Collins is brandy based and Pedro Collins is made with rum. This Irish whiskey cocktail is sometimes called Mick Collins.

Mike Collins

Put the ice cubes into a cocktail shaker. Pour the lemon juice, sugar syrup and whiskey over the ice and shake until a frost forms. Pour, without straining, into a tumbler or Collins glass and add the orange slice and cocktail cherry speared on a cocktail stick. Top up with soda water, stir lightly and serve decorated with an orange rind spiral.

5–6 ice cubes
juice of 1 lemon
1 tablespoon sugar syrup
(see page 12)
3 measures Irish whiskey
1 slice of orange
1 cocktail cherry
soda water
orange rind spiral, to decorate

🕐 Preparation time: 3 minutes

🍸 Serves 1

Walters

Put the ice cubes into a mixing glass. Pour the lemon juice, orange juice and whisky over the ice. Stir vigorously, then strain into a chilled old-fashioned glass. Serve decorated with an orange slice. Drink with a straw.

4–5 ice cubes
juice of ½ lemon
juice of ½ orange
3 measures bourbon or
    Scotch whisky
slice of orange, to decorate

🕐 Preparation time: 3 minutes
🍸 Serves 1

Club *left*

Put the ice into a mixing glass. Add the bitters then the whisky and grenadine. Stir well. Strain into a cocktail glass and decorate with the spiral of lemon and a cherry.

🕐 Preparation time: 3 minutes
🍸 Serves 1

3 ice cubes, cracked
2 dashes Angostura bitters
1 measure Scotch whisky
dash of grenadine
To Decorate:
lemon rind spiral
1 cocktail cherry

Rob Roy was both a historical character and the eponymous hero of a novel by Sir Walter Scott. A powerful and dangerous outlaw and a Jacobite sympathizer, he was also renowned for his kindness and generosity to the oppressed – a kind of Scottish Robin Hood and much-admired figure in Scottish folk history.

Rob Roy *right*

Put the ice cube, whisky, vermouth and bitters into a mixing glass and stir well. Strain into a cocktail glass and decorate the rim with the spiral of lemon.

🕐 Preparation time: 3 minutes
🍸 Serves 1

1 ice cube, cracked
1 measure Scotch whisky
½ measure dry vermouth
dash Angostura bitters
lemon rind spiral,
  to decorate

Golden Shot

Put the whisky, orange juice and egg yolk into a mixing glass and stir vigorously. Pour into an old-fashioned glass and decorate with the spiral of orange rind.

🕐 Preparation time: 3 minutes
🍸 Serves 1

1 measure whisky
3 measures fresh orange juice
1 egg yolk
orange rind spiral, to decorate

'God of the golden bow'
Apollo, Greek god of the sun, shines again
in this glowing cocktail.

Pancho Villa, whose first name was actually Francisco, was a Mexican revolutionary leader. He was assassinated in 1923 but has achieved immortality with this tequila cocktail.

Pancho Villa

Put the ice cubes into a cocktail shaker and pour in the tequila, Tia Maria and Cointreau. Shake until a frost forms, then strain into a chilled cocktail glass.

🕐 Preparation time: 3 minutes

🍸 Serves 1

4–5 ice cubes
1 measure tequila
½ measure Tia Maria
1 teaspoon Cointreau

Frostbite

Put the ice cubes into a cocktail shaker. Pour the tequila, cream and crème de cacao over the ice. Shake until a frost forms, then strain into a cocktail glass. Sprinkle with grated nutmeg.

🕐 Preparation time: 3 minutes
🍸 Serves 1

4–5 ice cubes
1 measure tequila
1 measure double cream
1 measure white crème
de cacao
grated nutmeg, to decorate

Azteca

Crush about half the ice cubes and put them into a blender. Add the tequila, lime juice, sugar syrup and mango and blend for a few seconds. Put the remaining ice cubes into a large cocktail glass then strain the drink over them. Decorate with the slice of lime and serve with short straws.

🕐 Preparation time: 3 minutes
🍸 Serves 1

8–10 ice cubes
1 measure tequila
juice of ½ lime
½ teaspoon sugar syrup (see
page 12)
1 small mango, peeled
and pitted
slice of lime, to decorate

'I'm pouring straight tequila over mixed emotion', – perhaps not the best recipe for a cocktail; or for coping with unhappiness.

81

Mad Dog

Put the ice cubes into a cocktail shaker. Pour the tequila, crème de banane, crème de cacao and lime juice over the ice and shake until a frost forms. Strain into a chilled cocktail glass and decorate with the lime slice, banana slice and cocktail cherry speared on a cocktail stick.

🕐 Preparation time: 3 minutes
🍸 Serves 1

4–5 ice cubes
1 measure tequila
1 measure crème de banane
1 measure crème de cacao
juice of ½ lime
To Decorate:
slice of lime
slice of banana
cocktail cherry

Gin has a very distinctive aroma of juniper and lingers on the breath. The Vodka Martini, sometimes known as a Vodkatini, became a popular, odour-free version among media people in the 1970s and 1980s, when the revived interest in cocktails had hit new heights.

Vodka Martini *right*

Put the ice cubes into a mixing glass. Pour the vermouth and vodka over the ice and stir vigorously, without splashing. Strain into a chilled cocktail glass, drop in the olive and serve.

4–5 ice cubes
¼ measure dry vermouth
3 measures vodka
1 green olive

🕐 Preparation time: 2 minutes
🍸 Serves 1

'A martini is an olive with an alcohol rub.'

Nerida

Put the ice cubes into a cocktail shaker. Pour the lime or lemon juice and whisky over the ice. Shake until a frost forms, then pour without straining into a chilled Collins glass. Top up with ginger ale and stir gently. Decorate with lime or lemon slices.

4–5 ice cubes
juice of ½ lime or lemon
3 measures Scotch whisky
dry ginger ale
slices of lime or lemon,
    to decorate

🕐 Preparation time: 3 minutes
🍸 Serves 1

Whisky Mac

Place the ice cubes in a large tumbler or old-fashioned glass. Pour over the whisky and ginger wine and stir.

2–3 ice cubes
1 measure Scotch whisky
1 measure ginger wine

🕐 Preparation time: 3 minutes
🍸 Serves 1

Benedict *left*

Put the ice cubes into a mixing glass. Pour the
Bénédictine and whisky over the ice. Stir evenly
without splashing and, without straining, pour
the cocktail into a chilled highball glass. Top up
with dry ginger ale and serve.

3–4 ice cubes
1 measure Bénédictine
3 measures Scotch whisky
dry ginger ale

🕐 Preparation time: 3 minutes
🍸 Serves 1

*'I slunk off in the direction of the
cocktail table – the only place in the
garden where a single man could linger
without looking purposeless and alone.'
Nick Carraway attends one of Jay Gatsby's
parties for the first time.*

85

Cassis Cocktail

Put the ice cubes into a cocktail shaker and pour in
the bourbon, vermouth and crème de cassis. Shake
the drink, then strain into a chilled cocktail glass
and decorate with the blueberries impaled on a
cocktail stick.

4–5 ice cubes
1 measure bourbon whiskey
½ measure dry vermouth
1 teaspoon crème de cassis
2 blueberries, to decorate

🕐 Preparation time: 3 minutes
🍸 Serves 1

Blueberries
As well as tasting delicious, blueberries can improve
your health as they have a high content of vitamins
A and C.

Ritz Old-Fashioned *top*

Dip the rim of an old-fashioned glass in the beaten egg white, then the caster sugar. Put the ice into a cocktail shaker and add the bourbon, Grand Marnier, lemon juice and bitters. Shake together, then strain into the glass. Decorate with the orange or lemon slice and the cherry.

🕐 Preparation time: 3 minutes

🍸 Serves 1

lightly beaten egg white
caster sugar, for rimming
3 ice cubes, crushed
1½ measures bourbon whiskey
½ measure Grand Marnier
dash of lemon juice
dash Angostura bitters
To Decorate:
1 slice of orange or lemon
1 cocktail cherry

Bourbon whiskey
Bourbon is aged in charred, white oak barrels; this produces a characteristically mellow whiskey.

86

New Yorker *bottom*

Put the ice cubes into a cocktail shaker and add the whisky, lime juice and sugar. Shake until a frost forms. Strain into a cocktail glass. Squeeze the zest from the lemon over the surface and decorate the rim with the spiral.

🕐 Preparation time: 3 minutes

🍸 Serves 1

2–3 ice cubes, cracked
1 measure Scotch whisky
1 teaspoon fresh lime juice
1 teaspoon powdered sugar
½ lemon
lemon rind spiral, to decorate

Batiste

Put the ice cubes into a mixing glass. Pour the
Grand Marnier and rum over the ice, stir vigorously
then strain into a cocktail glass.

4–5 ice cubes
1 measure Grand Marnier
2 measures golden or dark rum

🕐 Preparation time: 2 minutes
🍸 Serves 1

'Rum Ring Links Nation' –
American headline.

Cinnamon
Cinnamon is the thinly rolled bark of an evergreen tree that grows in India, Sri Lanka, Madagascar and the Caribbean. It has a slightly hot flavour and is perhaps best known for its use in mulled wine.

Grenada Cocktail

Put the ice cubes into a mixing glass. Pour the orange juice, vermouth and rum over the ice, stir vigorously then strain into a cocktail glass. Decorate with small pieces of cinnamon stick, if liked.

🕐 Preparation time: 2 minutes

🍸 Serves 1

4–5 ice cubes
juice of ½ orange
1 measure sweet vermouth
3 measures golden or dark rum
small pieces of cinnamon stick,
    to decorate (optional)

Black Russian *left*

Put some cracked ice into a short glass. Add
the vodka and Kahlúa and stir. Decorate with
a chocolate stick, if liked.

3 cracked ice cubes
2 measures vodka
1 measure Kahlúa
chocolate stick, to
    decorate (optional)

🕐 Preparation time: 2 minutes
🍸 Serves 1

*'This will last out a night
in Russia / When nights are longest
there.'*

White Russian *right*

Put half the ice cubes into a cocktail shaker and
add the vodka, Tia Maria and milk or double cream.
Shake to mix. Put the remaining ice cubes into a tall
narrow glass and strain the cocktail over them.
Drink with a straw.

5 cracked ice cubes
1 measure vodka
1 measure Tia Maria
1 measure milk or
    double cream

🕐 Preparation time: 3 minutes
🍸 Serves 1

90

October Revolution

Put half the ice cubes in a cocktail shaker. Pour
the vodka, Tia Maria, crème de cacao and cream
over the ice and shake until a frost forms. Put the
remaining ice into a tall narrow glass, strain the
cocktail over them and serve with a straw.

5 cracked ice cubes
1 measure vodka
1 measure Tia Maria
1 measure crème de cacao
1 measure double cream

🕐 Preparation time: 3 minutes
🍸 Serves 1

*'Revolutions are not
made with rosewater.'*

This is a variation of a cocktail from Brazil, made from cachaça – a blend of rum and sugar cane. It is very difficult to find outside South America, but a mixture of vodka and brown sugar or molasses makes a good substitute.

Caipirinha

Place 3 of the lime wedges in a large tumbler or old-fashioned glass and add the brown sugar and cachaça or vodka. Mix well, mashing the limes slightly to make a little juice. Top up with the crushed ice cubes and decorate with the remaining lime wedges.

6 lime wedges
2 teaspoons brown sugar
2 measures cachaça or vodka
4–5 ice cubes, crushed

🕐 Preparation time: 3 minutes
🍸 Serves 1

Black Widow

Put the ice cubes into a cocktail shaker. Pour in the rum, Southern Comfort, lime juice and sugar syrup and shake well. Strain into a chilled cocktail glass and decorate with a lime slice.

🕐 Preparation time: 3 minutes

🍸 Serves 1

4–5 ice cubes

2 measures dark rum

1 measure Southern Comfort

juice of ½ lime

dash of sugar syrup (see
      page 12)

slice of lime, to decorate

Southern Comfort
An American liqueur, Southern Comfort combines
the flavours of Bourbon whiskey, peaches, oranges
and herbs.

Xantippe was proverbially a nagging and shrewish woman.
Perhaps this golden concoction will sweeten her nature.

Xantippe

Put the ice cubes into a mixing glass. Pour the
cherry brandy, yellow Chartreuse and vodka
over the ice and stir vigorously. Strain into a
chilled cocktail glass.

4–5 ice cubes
1 measure cherry brandy
1 measure yellow Chartreuse
2 measures vodka

🕐 Preparation time: 2 minutes
🍸 Serves 1

Inspiration

Put the ice cubes into a mixing glass. Pour the Bénédictine, vermouth and vodka over the ice. Stir vigorously, then strain into a chilled cocktail glass and decorate with the lime spiral.

- Preparation time: 2 minutes
- Serves 1

4–5 ice cubes
½ measure Bénédictine
½ measure dry vermouth
2 measures vodka
1 lime rind spiral,
    to decorate

Lime spirals
Often used to decorate individual cocktail glasses, the lime spiral takes a good deal of practice to perfect, owing to its thin rind (see page 20).

Cool Wind

Put the ice cubes into a mixing glass. Pour the vermouth, grapefruit juice, Cointreau and vodka over the ice. Stir gently, then strain into a chilled cocktail glass.

- Preparation time: 2 minutes
- Serves 1

4–5 ice cubes
1 measure dry vermouth
juice of ½ grapefruit
½ teaspoon Cointreau
3 measures vodka

95

'For the gentle wind does move / Silently, invisibly' – in other words, stirred, not shaken.

Sirocco

Put the ice cubes into a cocktail shaker. Pour the crème de menthe, gin and vodka over the ice and shake until a frost forms. Strain into a chilled cocktail glass.

- Preparation time: 3 minutes
- Serves 1

4–5 ice cubes
½ measure crème de menthe
½ measure gin
2 measures vodka

*This is an enchanting cocktail that will have you spell bound –
it looks so harmless, but packs a powerful punch and tastes
absolutely magical.*

White Witch

Put 4–5 ice cubes into a cocktail shaker and pour in
the rum, crème de cacao, Cointreau and lime juice.
Put 4–5 fresh ice cubes into an old-fashioned glass.
Shake the drink, then strain it into the glass. Top up
with soda water and stir to mix. Decorate with slices
of orange and lime and serve with straws.

🕐 Preparation time: 3 minutes

🍸 Serves 1

8–10 ice cubes
1 measure white rum
½ measure white crème
de cacao
½ measure Cointreau
juice of ½ lime
soda water
To Decorate:
slice of orange
slice of lime

This is one cocktail where it is worth experimenting with flavoured vodkas. Try a fruity flavour, such as orange, lemon or peach, or one of the herb ones. The result will be affected by the aniseed taste of the Pernod, so choose with care.

Vodka Sazerac

Put the sugar cube into an old-fashioned glass and shake the bitters on to it. Add the Pernod to the glass and swirl it about so that it clings to the side of the glass. Drop in the ice cubes and pour in the vodka. Top up with lemonade, then stir gently and serve with a straw.

1 sugar cube
2 drops Angostura bitters
3 drops of Pernod
2–3 ice cubes
2 measures vodka
lemonade, to top up

🕐 Preparation time: 2 minutes

🍸 Serves 1

Brandy Sidecar *left*

Put the ice cubes into a mixing glass. Pour the lemon juice, Cointreau and brandy over the ice and stir vigorously. Strain into a chilled cocktail glass. Decorate with orange rind and a cocktail cherry on a cocktail stick.

🕐 Preparation time: 2 minutes
🍸 Serves 1

4–5 ice cubes
juice of 1 lemon
1 measure Cointreau
2 measures brandy
To Decorate:
orange rind
cocktail cherry

'Brandy is a cordial composed one part thunder-and-lightning, one part remorse, two parts bloody murder, one part death-hell-and-the grave and four parts clarified Satan.'

There is no medical evidence whatsoever to suggest that 'a hair of the dog' will cure a hangover or, indeed, that brandy can cure any malady at all, but when you feel like the living dead, this cocktail might just work the trick.

99

Corpse Reviver

Put the ice cubes into a cocktail shaker and pour in the brandy, Fernet Branca and crème de menthe. Shake until a frost forms, then strain into a chilled cocktail glass.

🕐 Preparation time: 3 minutes
🍸 Serves 1

4–5 ice cubes
1 measure brandy
1 measure Fernet Branca
1 measure white crème
  de menthe

Fernet Branca
An Italian bitters distilled from alpine herbs and flavoured, originally, with the bark of a Bolivian tree, Fernet Branca has a reputation for curing a queasy stomach, especially when caused by a hangover. It is very bitter.

Brandy Cuban

Place the ice cubes in a tumbler and pour over the brandy and lime juice. Stir vigorously to mix. Top up with cola and decorate with a slice of lime. Serve with a straw.

🕐 Preparation time: 2 minutes

🍸 Serves 1

2–3 ice cubes
1½ measures brandy
juice of ½ lime
cola, to top up
slice of lime, to decorate

Baltimore Egg Nog

Put the ice cubes into a cocktail shaker. Add the egg, sugar syrup, brandy, rum, Madeira and milk and shake well until a frost forms. Strain into a goblet and sprinkle with cinnamon. Serve with a cinnamon stick.

🕐 Preparation time: 3 minutes

🍸 Serves 1

4–5 ice cubes

1 egg

1 tablespoon sugar syrup (see page 12)

½ measure brandy

½ measure dark rum

½ measure Madeira

2 measures milk

To Decorate:

ground cinnamon

cinnamon stick

Madeira
Madeira is a fortified wine from the island of the same name.

Paradise *right*

Put the ice cubes into a cocktail shaker. Add the lemon juice, orange juice, gin and apricot brandy and shake together. Strain into a chilled cocktail glass and decorate with slices of lemon and orange.

🕐 Preparation time: 3 minutes
🍸 Serves 1

4–5 ice cubes
dash of fresh lemon juice
1 measure fresh orange juice
1 measure gin
1 measure apricot brandy
To Decorate:
slice of lemon
slice of orange

'…And drunk the milk of Paradise.' The poet Coleridge warns of the consequences in Kubla Khan.

Heir Apparent

Put the ice cubes into a mixing glass. Shake the bitters over the ice and pour in the brandy. Stir vigorously, then strain into a chilled cocktail glass. Add the crème de menthe and serve decorated with the mint sprig.

🕐 Preparation time: 2 minutes
🍸 Serves 1

4–5 ice cubes
3 drops orange bitters or
    Angostura bitters
3 measures brandy
3 drops of white crème de menthe
sprig of mint, to decorate

102

'…for weeks they had drunk cocktails before meals like Americans, wines and brandies like Frenchmen, beer like Germans, whisky-and-soda like the English'. Scott Fitzgerald defines the drinking habits of the 'Lost Generation'.

For a really fruity flavour, it is worth buying orange bitters rather than Angostura. For a Burnt Sienna, substitute peach bitters and peach juice for the orange.

Burnt Orange *right*

Put the ice cubes into a mixing glass. Shake the bitters over the ice, add the orange juice and brandy and stir vigorously. Strain into a chilled cocktail glass and serve decorated with an orange slice.

4–5 ice cubes
3 drops orange bitters or
    Angostura bitters
juice of ½ orange
3 measures brandy
slice of orange, to decorate

🕐 Preparation time: 2 minutes
🍸 Serves 1

'A man takes a drink, the *drink takes another and the drink takes the man.'*

Toulon

Put the ice cubes into a mixing glass. Pour the vermouth, Bénédictine and brandy over the ice and stir vigorously. Strain into a chilled cocktail glass and decorate with the orange rind.

4–5 ice cubes
1 measure dry vermouth
1 measure Bénédictine
3 measures brandy
piece of orange rind,
    to decorate

🕐 Preparation time: 2 minutes
🍸 Serves 1

Caen-Caen

Put the ice into a mixing glass. Pour the brandy, Calvados and sweet vermouth over the ice and stir vigorously. Strain into a cocktail glass.

4–5 ice cubes
2 measures brandy
1 measure Calvados
½ measure sweet vermouth

🕐 Preparation time: 2 minutes
🍸 Serves 1

The dryness of the gin and vermouth in this cocktail is counterbalanced by the sweetness of the cherry brandy. A similar cocktail, Sleeping Beauty, can be made with strawberry-flavoured crème de fraises de bois.

Red Kiss

Put the ice cubes into a mixing glass, add the vermouth, gin and cherry brandy and stir well. Strain into a chilled cocktail glass and decorate with the cherry and spiral of lemon.

3 ice cubes, cracked
1 measure dry vermouth
½ measure gin
½ measure cherry brandy
To Decorate:
1 cocktail cherry
lemon rind spiral

🕐 Preparation time: 3 minutes
🍸 Serves 1

Woodstock

Put the ice into a cocktail shaker and add the gin, vermouth, Cointreau and orange juice. Shake to mix then strain into a chilled cocktail glass. Squeeze the zest from the orange rind over the surface and decorate with the slice of orange twisted over the rim of the glass.

2–3 ice cubes, crushed
1 measure gin
1 measure dry vermouth
¼ measure Cointreau
1 measure fresh orange juice
To Decorate:
piece of orange rind
slice of orange

🕐 Preparation time: 3 minutes
🍸 Serves 1

Sweet Sixteen

Put half the ice cubes into a cocktail shaker. Pour the gin, lime juice, grenadine and sugar syrup over the ice and shake until a frost forms. Place the remaining ice in a highball glass, strain the cocktail over the ice and top up with bitter lemon. Decorate with the lemon rind.

6–8 ice cubes
2 measures gin
juice of ½ lime
2 dashes grenadine
1 teaspoon sugar syrup
   (see page 12)
bitter lemon, to top up
strip of lemon rind, to decorate

🕐 Preparation time: 3 minutes
🍸 Serves 1

107

Sadly, this prettily named cocktail has nothing to do with weddings or even flowers. Also known as Adirondack, it dates from the years of Prohibition. The orange juice was designed to disguise the foul taste of a hearty measure of bath-tub gin.

Orange Blossom

Pour the gin, vermouth and orange juice into a cocktail shaker and shake to mix. Place the ice cubes in a tall glass and strain the cocktail over them. Decorate with the slice of orange twisted over the rim of the glass.

1 measure gin
1 measure sweet vermouth
1 measure fresh orange juice
1–2 ice cubes
slice of orange, to decorate

🕐 Preparation time: 3 minutes
🍸 Serves 1

Crème de banane is a very strongly flavoured and quite sweet liqueur, so it can be overpowering. This is deliciously counter-balanced by the richness of the brandy and the orange of the Cointreau in this cocktail.

Banana Bliss

Put the ice cubes into a mixing glass and pour in the brandy, crème de banane and Cointreau. Stir with a spoon, then strain into a cocktail glass. Dip the banana into lemon juice to prevent it discolouring, then attach it to the rim of the glass.

4–5 ice cubes
1 measure brandy
1 measure crème de banane
1 measure Cointreau
slice of banana
fresh lemon juice

🕐 Preparation time: 3 minutes
🍸 Serves 1

This is yet another member of the prolific Alexander family. Still based on brandy, it is flavoured with Kahlúa, giving it a rich coffee aroma and taste.

Alexander's Sister

Put the ice cubes into a cocktail shaker. Pour the brandy, Kahlúa and cream over the ice cubes and shake well. Strain into a cocktail glass and sprinkle with grated nutmeg.

4–5 ice cubes
1 measure brandy
1 measure Kahlúa
1 measure double cream
grated nutmeg

🕐 Preparation time: 3 minutes
🍸 Serves 1

Depth Bomb

Put the ice cubes into a mixing glass. Pour the lemon juice, grenadine, Calvados and brandy over the ice and stir vigorously. Strain into a chilled cocktail glass and decorate with slices of apple.

4–5 ice cubes
juice of 1 lemon
½ teaspoon grenadine
1 measure Calvados
2 measures brandy
slices of red- or green-
    skinned apple, to decorate

🕐 Preparation time: 2 minutes
🍸 Serves 1

109

'Ban the bomb.' This Pacifist *slogan from the Cold War years should not be applied to cocktails.*

Bouncing Bomb

Put the ice cubes into a mixing glass. Pour the brandy and Curaçao over the ice and stir vigorously. Strain into a highball glass and top up with soda water. Decorate with the orange rind.

4–5 ice cubes
2 measures brandy
1 measure Curaçao
soda water, to top up
strip of orange rind,
    to decorate

🕐 Preparation time: 2 minutes
🍸 Serves 1

Monta Rosa *left*

Put the ice cubes into a mixing glass. Pour the lime juice, Cointreau and brandy over the ice and stir vigorously. Strain into a chilled cocktail glass.

🕐 Preparation time: 2 minutes
🍸 Serves 1

4–5 ice cubes
juice of ½ lime
1 measure Cointreau
3 measures brandy

Flips usually contain a whole egg, which is either beaten or shaken or both. They can be flavoured with a wide variety of liqueurs and, although other spirits can be used as the base, brandy is by far the most common.

Coffee Flip *right*

Put 4–5 ice cubes into a cocktail shaker. Pour in the brandy, Kahlúa, cream and sugar syrup, then add the egg, coffee and milk and shake well for 45 seconds. Put the remaining ice cubes into a tall glass, strain the drink over the ice and sprinkle with ground coriander.

🕐 Preparation time: 3 minutes
🍸 Serves 1

8–10 ice cubes
1 measure brandy
1 measure Kahlúa
2 teaspoons double cream
1½ teaspoons sugar syrup (see page 12)
1 egg, beaten
½ teaspoon instant coffee
125 ml (4 fl oz) milk
ground coriander, to decorate

Invalid's Egg Flip

Put the egg yolk, sugar syrup, brandy and port into a cocktail shaker and shake well to mix. Pour into a heatproof glass, top up with the hot milk and sprinkle with nutmeg.

🕐 Preparation time: 4 minutes
🍸 Serves 1

1 egg yolk
1 teaspoon sugar syrup (see page 12)
1 measure brandy
1 measure port
150 ml (¼ pint) hot milk
grated nutmeg, to decorate

The classic Manhattan cocktail is made with whiskey, usually rye but sometimes with bourbon. This is a brandy-based variation. Traditionally, it is always decorated with a cherry.

Brandy Manhattan

Put the ice cubes into a mixing glass. Pour the vermouth and brandy over the ice and stir vigorously. Pour into a chilled glass and decorate with the cocktail cherry.

4–5 ice cubes
1 measure sweet vermouth
3 measures brandy
1 cocktail cherry, to decorate

🕐 Preparation time: 2 minutes
🍸 Serves 1

Horse's Neck was so called because it is traditionally decorated with a long spiral of lemon rind. The spirit on which the cocktail is based varies. Brandy is the most popular choice in Britain, but bourbon whiskey is widely used in the United States. Sometimes it is even made with gin.

Horse's Neck

Put the ice into a tall glass and pour over the brandy. Top up with ginger ale. Hang the spiral of lemon over the rim to decorate.

3 ice cubes, cracked
1½ measures brandy
ginger ale, to top up
spiral of lemon rind,
to decorate

🕐 Preparation time: 2 minutes
🍸 Serves 1

The name alone should warn you to handle this mixture with caution – it has a wicked sting in the tail.

Scorpion

Put half the ice into a cocktail shaker and add the brandy, white and dark rums, orange juice, Amaretto and bitters. Shake until a frost forms. Put the remaining ice into a tall glass or goblet and strain the cocktail over it. Decorate with the orange or lemon slices and drink with a straw.

5 ice cubes, crushed
1 measure brandy
½ measure white rum
½ measure dark rum
2 measures fresh orange juice
2 teaspoons Amaretto di Saronno
2–3 dashes Angostura bitters
slices of orange or lemon,
to decorate

🕐 Preparation time: 3 minutes
🍸 Serves 1

113

Prairie Oyster

Put the brandy, egg yolk, vinegar, Tabasco and Worcestershire sauces and cayenne into a wine glass. Stir gently without breaking the egg yolk.

2 measures brandy
1 egg yolk
1 teaspoon wine vinegar
dash of Tabasco sauce
dash of Worcestershire sauce
pinch of cayenne pepper

🕐 Preparation time: 2 minutes
🍸 Serves 1

Tall Drinks

Long, cold and effervescent, coolers and fizzers are the perfect cocktails for quenching the thirst on warm summer evenings. Fruit juice, soda water, wine and Champagne blend with the spirits to create lively, taste-bud tingling cocktails and punches. From the traditional Classic Pimm's and the tropical Hawaiian Vodka to the frivolous Morning Glory Fizz and decadent Blue Champagne, there is something to please everyone. These are the ideal drinks to enjoy with friends or, alternatively, find a quiet spot, relax, and feel the tensions of the day slip away as you sip one of these cool concoctions!

Classic Pimm's *right*

Pour the Pimm's into a hurricane or highball glass and add the ice cubes. Add the fruit and cucumber slices, then add the lemonade. Decorate with mint or borage and drink with a straw, if liked.

🕐 Preparation time: 3 minutes
🍸 Serves 1

1 measure Pimm's No 1 cup
3–4 ice cubes
2–3 slices of orange, lemon
    and cucumber
3 measures lemonade
sprigs of mint or borage,
    to decorate (optional)

Borage
Borage has large pale green hairy leaves, and small bright blue star-shaped flowers, both of which have a faint flavour reminiscent of cucumber. Its most common use is as a decoration for Pimm's and other wine-based cups.

116

St James

Put the ice cubes into a highball glass and pour in the lime or lemon juice and the orange juice. Shake the bitters on the ice, add the rum and tonic water and decorate with a lime or lemon slice. Stir gently and serve.

🕐 Preparation time: 2 minutes
🍸 Serves 1

3–4 ice cubes
juice of ½ lime or lemon
juice of 1 orange
3 drops Angostura bitters
2 measures white or golden rum
2 measures tonic water
slice of lime or lemon

Tonic Water
Often simply known as tonic, this is a carbonated, non-alcoholic beverage, flavoured with quinine and used as a mixer. It is most often associated with gin-based drinks.

Vodka Twister Fizz *left*

Put the ice cubes into a cocktail shaker. Pour the lemon juice, sugar syrup, egg white, Pernod and vodka over the ice and shake until a frost forms. Pour, without straining, into a highball glass and top up with ginger ale. Stir once or twice, decorate with a lime slice and serve.

🕐 Preparation time: 2 minutes

🍸 Serves 1

4–5 ice cubes

juice of 1 lemon

½ teaspoon sugar syrup (see page 12)

1 egg white

3 drops of Pernod

3 measures vodka

ginger ale, to top up

slice of lime, to decorate

It is anyone's guess whether the title of this cocktail refers to the Antipodes, the effect of downing several glasses in succession or its pick-me-up effect on depressed spirits. In fact, the cocktail and its pale peachy colouring remain 'down under' the colourless soda water, as it is not stirred after topping up.

Down-under Fizz *right*

Put the ice cubes into a cocktail shaker. Pour the lemon and orange juices, grenadine and vodka over the ice and shake until a frost forms. Pour, without straining, into a Collins glass and top up with soda water. Serve with a straw.

🕐 Preparation time: 3 minutes

🍸 Serves 1

4–5 ice cubes

juice of 1 lemon

juice of ½ orange

½ teaspoon grenadine

3 measures vodka

soda water, to top up

Fresh Fields

Put the ice cubes into a cocktail shaker. Pour the vodka and kümmel over the ice and shake until a frost forms. Pour, without straining, into a highball glass and top up with soda water. Stir gently and decorate with a slice of lemon.

🕐 Preparation time: 3 minutes

🍸 Serves 1

4–5 ice cubes

2 measures vodka

1 measure kümmel

soda water, to top up

slice of lemon, to decorate

Astronaut *right*

Put 4–5 ice cubes into a cocktail shaker and add the rum, vodka, lemon and passion fruit juices. Fill an old-fashioned glass with 4–5 fresh ice cubes. Shake the drink, then strain it into the glass. Decorate with the lemon wedge.

🕐 Preparation time: 3 minutes

🍸 Serves 1

8–10 ice cubes
½ measure white rum
½ measure vodka
½ measure fresh lemon juice
dash of passion fruit juice
lemon wedge, to decorate

Zombies contain all three types of rum – dark, golden and white. Dark rum is aged in charred oak casks, while white rum is aged in stainless steel tanks.

Havana Zombie

Put the ice cubes into a mixing glass. Pour the lime juice and pineapple juice, sugar syrup and rums over the ice and stir vigorously. Pour, without straining, into a tall glass.

🕐 Preparation time: 2 minutes

🍸 Serves 1

4–5 ice cubes
juice of 1 lime
5 tablespoons pineapple juice
1 teaspoon sugar syrup (see page 12)
1 measure white rum
1 measure golden rum
1 measure dark rum

Ragged Island Zombie

Put the ice cubes into a mixing glass. Pour the lime juice, sugar syrup, rums and orange liqueur over the ice and stir vigorously. Pour, without straining, into a chilled glass.

🕐 Preparation time: 2 minutes

🍸 Serves 1

4–5 ice cubes
juice of 1 lime
1 teaspoon sugar syrup (see page 12)
1 measure white rum
½ measure golden rum
½ measure dark rum
1 measure Nassau orange

'He took another cocktail – not because he needed confidence but because she had given him so much of it.'

Sugar is one of Hawaii's main crops, so perhaps it is surprising that the best-known cocktail of the name is based on vodka, rather than rum. On the other hand, pineapples are the other main crop of this group of tropical islands …

Hawaiian Vodka

Put the ice cubes into a cocktail shaker. Pour the pineapple, lemon and orange juices, grenadine and vodka over the ice and shake until a frost forms. Strain into a tumbler and decorate with a slice of lemon. Drink with a straw.

🕐 Preparation time: 3 minutes

🍸 Serves 1

4–5 ice cubes
1 measure pineapple juice
juice of 1 lemon
juice of 1 orange
1 teaspoon grenadine
3 measures vodka
slice of lemon, to decorate

Gin Tropical   *above*

Put 4–5 ice cubes into a cocktail shaker, pour in
the gin, lemon juice, passion fruit juice and orange
juice and shake well. Put 4–5 fresh ice cubes into
an old-fashioned glass and strain the cocktail over
the ice. Top up with soda water and stir gently.
Decorate with an orange rind spiral.

🕐 Preparation time: 3 minutes
🍸 Serves 1

8–10 ice cubes
1½ measures gin
1 measure fresh lemon juice
1 measure passion fruit juice
½ measure fresh orange juice
soda water
orange rind spiral, to decorate

Zaza

Put the ice cubes into a mixing glass. Shake the
bitters over the ice, pour in the Dubonnet and gin
and stir vigorously without splashing. Strain into a
chilled cocktail glass.

🕐 Preparation time: 3 minutes
🍸 Serves 1

5–6 ice cubes
3 drops of orange bitters
1 measure Dubonnet
2 measures gin

The word punch is thought to derive from panch, *Hindi for five, as that was originally the number of ingredients. These days, punch has become more elaborate and may have any number of ingredients.*

Punch Julien *left*

Pour the lime juice and pineapple juice into a mixing glass and dash in the bitters. Pour in the grenadine and golden and dark rums and add the fruit. Stir thoroughly then chill in the refrigerator for 3 hours. Fill an old-fashioned glass with cracked ice. Pour the punch over the ice and add the fruit. Sprinkle with nutmeg and serve decorated with a pineapple wedge.

🕐 Preparation time: 3 minutes, plus chilling
🍸 Serves 1

juice of 2 limes
1 measure unsweetened
    pineapple juice
3 drops Angostura bitters
½ teaspoon grenadine
1 measure golden rum
3 measures dark rum
slice of lime
slice of lemon
slice of orange
grated nutmeg
1 pineapple wedge, plus extra
    to decorate

Bahamas Punch *right*

Pour the lemon juice and sugar syrup into a mixing glass. Shake in the bitters, then add the grenadine, rum and orange and lemon slices. Stir thoroughly then chill for 3 hours. To serve, fill an old-fashioned glass with cracked ice, pour in the punch without straining and sprinkle with nutmeg.

🕐 Preparation time: 3 minutes, plus chilling
🍸 Serves 1

juice of 1 lemon
1 teaspoon sugar syrup (see
    page 12)
3 drops of Angostura bitters
½ teaspoon grenadine
3 measures golden or white rum
slice of orange
slice of lemon
cracked ice
grated nutmeg

Brazilian Punch

Pour the mango juice, brandy and rum into a mixing glass and add the slices of fruit. Stir thoroughly and chill in the refrigerator for 3 hours. To serve, fill an old-fashioned glass with cracked ice and pour in the punch without straining.

🕐 Preparation time: 3 minutes, plus chilling
🍸 Serves 1

2 measures mango juice
1 measure brandy
2 measures dark rum
slice of lime
slice of lemon
slice of orange
cracked ice

Long, cold and effervescent, fizzes are the perfect cocktails for quenching the thirst on warm summer evenings.

Morning Glory Fizz

Put the ice cubes into a cocktail shaker. Pour the lemon juice, sugar syrup and gin over the ice. Add the egg white, then the Pernod and shake until a frost forms. Strain into a chilled old-fashioned glass, top up with ginger ale and serve with a straw.

🕐 Preparation time: 3 minutes

🍸 Serves 1

4–5 ice cubes

1 measure fresh lemon juice

½ teaspoon sugar syrup (see page 12)

3 measures gin

1 egg white

3 drops of Pernod

ginger ale

For authenticity, use Haitian rum, which at its best, is said to be phenomenal. The island produces both light and dark rums of legendary potency.

Zombie Prince

Put the crushed ice into a mixing glass. Pour the lemon, orange and grapefruit juices over the ice and splash in the bitters. Add the sugar and pour in the three rums. Stir vigorously, then pour, without straining, into a Collins glass. Decorate with lime and orange slices.

● Preparation time: 3 minutes

🍸 Serves 1

crushed ice
juice of 1 lemon
juice of 1 orange
juice of ½ grapefruit
3 drops Angostura bitters
1 teaspoon soft brown sugar
1 measure white rum
1 measure golden rum
1 measure dark rum
To Decorate:
slices of lime
slice of orange

Julep means syrup and any version of this cocktail is always very sweet, but the mint adds a pungency that prevents it from tasting too sugary.

Virginia Mint Julep

Put the mint sprigs into an iced silver mug or tall glass. Add the sugar syrup, then crush the mint into the syrup with a teaspoon. Fill the mug or glass with dry crushed ice, pour the whiskey over the ice and stir gently. Pack in more crushed ice and stir until a frost forms. Wrap the mug or glass in a table napkin and serve decorated with a mint sprig.

9 tender sprigs of young mint, plus extra, to decorate
1 teaspoon sugar syrup (see page 12)
crushed ice
3 measures bourbon whiskey

🕐 Preparation time: 3 minutes
🍸 Serves 1

This potent mix is refreshing on a hot summer's evening, but it might be wise to avoid playing poker with strangers after one or two glasses.

Mississippi Punch

Half-fill a tall glass with crushed ice. Shake the bitters over the ice. Pour in the sugar syrup and the lemon juice, then stir gently to mix thoroughly. Add the brandy, rum and whiskey, in that order, stir once and serve with straws.

🕐 Preparation time: 3 minutes

🍸 Serves 1

crushed ice
3 drops Angostura bitters
1 teaspoon sugar syrup (see page 12)
juice of 1 lemon
1 measure brandy
1 measure dark rum
2 measures bourbon whiskey

Also known as cassis au vin blanc, this is a popular French aperitif made from the blackcurrant-flavoured liqueur, crème de cassis, and white wine. For a Kir Royale, substitute Champagne for ordinary white wine.

Kir *left*

Put the ice cubes into a goblet or old-fashioned glass. Pour the crème de cassis and wine over the ice, stir gently and serve.

2–3 ice cubes
1 measure crème de cassis
4 measures dry white wine

🕐 Preparation time: 2 minutes
🍸 Serves 1

'Good wine is a familiar creature if it be well used.'

Whenever a cocktail includes fruit juice, it is always better to use freshly squeezed juice. However, juice from bottles or cartons will still produce a tasty drink.

131

Acapulco Gold

Put 4–5 ice cubes into a cocktail shaker. Pour in the rum, tequila, pineapple and grapefruit juices and cream of coconut and shake until a frost forms. To serve, put 4–5 fresh ice cubes into an old-fashioned glass and strain the cocktail over the ice.

8–10 ice cubes
½ measure golden rum
½ measure tequila
1 measure pineapple juice
½ measure fresh grapefruit juice
½ measure cream of coconut

🕐 Preparation time: 3 minutes
🍸 Serves 1

Cream of Coconut
This is widely available from supermarkets and Chinese food stores. It may be sweetened or unsweetened.

Riesling is a variety of grape from which wines are made in many countries. It produces a light, flowery white wine that is perfect for hot summer days and ideal for this Summer Cup. Combine it with a light red wine, such as Beaujolais, and serve well chilled.

Summer Cup *left*

Pour the Riesling, red wine and Drambuie into a large chilled bowl. Add the lemonade, fruit and ice cubes. Serve as soon as possible in glasses decorated with strawberry slices.

🕐 Preparation time: 3 minutes
🍸 Serves 15

1 bottle Riesling, chilled
1 bottle light red wine
75 ml (3 fl oz) Drambuie
750 ml (1¼ pints) lemonade, chilled
1 dessert apple, sliced
1 orange, sliced
a few strawberries, halved
ice cubes
slices of strawberry, to decorate

Honeysuckle Cup *right*

Put the honey into a large bowl and gradually stir in the wine. Add the Bénédictine and brandy. Chill for 2 hours. Just before serving, add the lemonade and fruit.

🕐 Preparation time: 10 minutes, plus chilling
🍸 Serves 10–12

1 tablespoon clear honey
1 bottle medium dry white wine
2 tablespoons Bénédictine
150 ml (¼ pint) brandy
750 ml (1¼ pints) lemonade
1 peach, skinned and sliced
seasonal fruit, to decorate

Jonathan's Joy

Put the ice into a cocktail shaker. Pour the Calvados and Cointreau over the ice and shake until a frost forms. Pour into a tall glass and top up with cider. Decorate with a slice of apple.

🕐 Preparation time: 3 minutes
🍸 Serves 1

4–5 ice cubes
2 measures Calvados
1 measure Cointreau
dry cider, to top up
slice of apple, to decorate

'Stay me with flagons,
comfort me with apples.'

Taking its name from sangre, *Spanish for blood, this fruit cup is usually based on red wine, but can also be made with white wine. Brandy or another spirit is often included, making it more potent than it seems at first sip.*

Sangria

Put the ice into a large bowl and pour over the wine and brandy, if using. Stir. Add soda water to taste and float the fruit on top. Serve in glasses decorated with an orange slice.

🕐 Preparation time: 8 minutes
🍸 Serves 10–12

ice cubes

2 bottles light Spanish red wine, chilled

125 ml (4 fl oz) brandy (optional)

about 450 ml (¾ pint) soda water, chilled

slices of seasonal fruit, such as apples, pears, oranges, lemons, peaches and strawberries

slices of orange, to decorate

Chablis Cup

Put the peaches, orange slices, cherries and sugar into a punch bowl. Pour in the chablis, Grand Marnier and kirsch and stir thoroughly. Cover the bowl and chill in the refrigerator for 1 hour. To serve, ladle into goblets.

🕐 Preparation time: 10 minutes, plus chilling
🍸 Serves 8

3 ripe peaches, skinned and sliced
1 orange, cut into thin slices
8 cocktail cherries
3 teaspoons sugar
1 bottle chablis
4 measures Grand Marnier
4 measures kirsch

A remarkably potent wine cup, this was described in an early twentieth-century cocktail book as something which 'definitely hits the spot'. Zut alors!

French '75 *left*

Half fill a tall glass with cracked ice. Add the gin, lemon juice and sugar and stir well. Top up with chilled Champagne or sparkling wine. Decorate with a slice of orange and cocktail cherries.

🕐 Preparation time: 2 minutes

🍸 Serves 1

6–8 cracked ice cubes
1 measure gin
juice of ½ lemon
1 teaspoon caster sugar
chilled Champagne or sparkling
    dry white wine, to top up
To Decorate:
slice of orange
cocktail cherries

Bellini *right*

Mix all the ingredients in a large wine glass and serve decorated with a peach slice and raspberries on a cocktail stick.

🕐 Preparation time: 2 minutes

🍸 Serves 1

2 measures unsweetened
    peach juice (preferably fresh)
4 measures chilled Champagne
    or sparking dry white wine
1 dash of grenadine (optional)
To Decorate:
slice of peach
raspberries

Whippersnapper

Put the peaches, apples, ginger and 2 tablespoons of the wine into a blender and blend briefly. Divide between 4 chilled tumblers, top up with the remaining wine and decorate with apple slices.

🕐 Preparation time: 4 minutes

🍸 Serves 4

2 peaches, skinned, pitted
    and chopped
2 small dessert apples, peeled,
    cored and chopped
2 teaspoons chopped
    stem ginger
1 bottle sparkling rosé wine
16–20 ice cubes
4 slices of apple, to decorate

Tall Drinks

This is based on the classic Bellini, but has a powerful kick, as most of the flavouring is derived from schnapps, rather than fruit juice. Schnapps is a Scandinavian spirit distilled from grain or potatoes and is produced in a variety of flavours.

Bellininitini *left*

Pour the vodka, peach schnapps and peach juice into a cocktail shaker. Shake thoroughly. Pour into a cocktail glass and top up with Champagne. Decorate with the slices of peach.

2 measures vodka
½ measure peach schnapps
1 teaspoon peach juice
chilled Champagne, to top up
slices of peach, to decorate

🕐 Preparation time: 3 minutes
🍸 Serves 1

'*The Norwegians live to eat and the Danes eat to live, while the Swedes eat to drink.*'

Blue Champagne *right*

Swirl the Curaçao around the sides of a champagne flute or wine glass to coat. Pour in the Champagne and serve.

4 dashes blue Curaçao
125 ml (4 fl oz) chilled Champagne
or sparkling white wine

🕐 Preparation time: 2 minutes
🍸 Serves 1

'*We can drink 'till all look blue.*' Playwright John Ford was not aware that you could start out with all brilliantly blue.

Pernod Fizz *left*

Put the Pernod into a champagne flute and swirl
it round to coat the sides. Slowly pour in the iced
Champagne, allowing the drink to become cloudy.
Decorate with a slice of lime.

🕐 Preparation time: 2 minutes
🍸 Serves 1

1 measure Pernod
175 ml (6 fl oz) chilled Champagne
slice of lime, to decorate

Brooklyn Bomber *right*

Put half the ice cubes into a cocktail shaker and
add the tequila, Curaçao, cherry brandy, Galliano
and lemon juice. Shake to mix. Put the remaining
ice into a hurricane glass or tall glass and pour the
drink over it. Decorate with the slice of orange and
cherries and drink with a straw.

🕐 Preparation time: 3 minutes
🍸 Serves 1

5 ice cubes, crushed
½ measure tequila
½ measure Curaçao
½ measure cherry brandy
½ measure Galliano
1 measure lemon juice
To Decorate:
slice of orange
2 cocktail cherries

140

*For more than 200 years, this has been the speciality of a
fishing club in Pennsylvania, called the State of Schuylkill.*

Fish House Punch

Put the lemon juice and sugar in a large punch bowl
and stir until the sugar has dissolved. Add the rum,
brandy, bitters, water and peaches and stir well to
mix. Chill for about 3 hours, stirring occasionally.
To serve, add ice cubes to the punch bowl, stir and
ladle into glasses.

🕐 Preparation time: 10 minutes, plus chilling
🍸 Serves 15–20

600 ml (1 pint) lemon juice
300 g (10 oz) brown sugar
1½ bottles dark rum
¾ bottle brandy
150 ml (¼ pint) peach bitters
1.5 litres (2½ pints) water
2–3 peaches, skinned, stoned
     and roughly chopped
ice cubes

Exotic Cocktails

These are drinks that will appeal as much to the eye as they do to the tastebuds. There are blue drinks and green drinks, layered drinks and drinks that defy gravity, and a stylish flaming drink that gives a performance worthy of an Oscar. The names of many of them are as exotic and intriguing as the ingredients: get your tongue round Ben's Orange Cream or Juliana Blue, and test the waters with Clear Skies Ahead or Havana Beach. You'll never be the same once you've tried your hand at some of these, and we think you'll agree that life will seem better and, definitely, brighter.

Not strictly a Martini, as it is not mixed with any kind of vermouth, this is still a spectacular drink. For a Topaz Martini, use golden Curaçao.

Sapphire Martini

Put the ice cubes into a cocktail shaker. Pour in the gin and blue Curaçao. Shake well to mix. Strain into a cocktail glass and carefully drop in a cocktail cherry, if using.

ice cubes

2 measures gin

½ measure blue Curaçao

1 red or blue cocktail cherry,
	to decorate (optional)

🕐 Preparation time: 3 minutes

🍸 Serves 1

Ben's Orange Cream

Put the ice cubes into a cocktail shaker. Pour the
Cointreau, cream and gin over the ice. Add the
sugar syrup and shake until a frost forms. Pour into
a large glass and decorate with a chocolate flake.

4–5 ice cubes

1 measure Cointreau

1 measure single cream

3 measures gin

1 tablespoon sugar syrup (see
    page 12)

chocolate flake, to decorate

🕐 Preparation time: 3 minutes

🍸 Serves 1

This cocktail is redolent of the long-gone and highly privileged days of colonialism – for some, at least – when meeting at the club on a warm summer's evening was the invariable prelude to a fine dinner.

Singapore Gin Sling

Put 4–6 ice cubes into a cocktail shaker. Pour the lemon and orange juices, cherry brandy and gin over the ice and add the bitters. Shake the mixture until a frost forms. Put 2 fresh ice cubes into a hurricane glass. Pour the cocktail, without straining, into the glass and top up with soda water. Decorate with the lemon slice and serve.

6–8 ice cubes
juice of ½ lemon
juice of ½ orange
1 measure cherry brandy
3 measures gin
3 drops Angostura bitters
soda water, to top up
slice of lemon, to decorate

🕐 Preparation time: 3 minutes
🍸 Serves 1

'The slings and arrows of outrageous fortune' – in this case, quite obviously, good fortune.

This cocktail could be described as a distant relative of the Collins family, possibly with a foreign connection.

Collinson

Put the ice cubes into a mixing glass, then add the bitters, gin, vermouth and kirsch. Stir well and strain into a cocktail glass. Squeeze the zest from the lemon rind over the surface and decorate the rim of the glass with the strawberry and lemon.

3 cracked ice cubes
dash of orange bitters
1 measure gin
½ measure dry vermouth
¼ measure kirsch
piece of lemon rind
To Decorate:
½ strawberry
slice of lemon

🕐 Preparation time: 2 minutes
🍸 Serves 1

Totally tropical – is that the rustle of the breeze in the palm trees or the shaking of grass-skirted hips? This delicious cocktail is a full measure of island hospitality.

Honolulu

Put the ice cubes into a cocktail shaker. Pour the pineapple, lemon and orange juices, the grenadine and gin over the ice and shake until a frost forms. Strain the drink into a chilled cocktail glass and decorate with the pineapple and cherry.

🕐 Preparation time: 3 minutes

🍸 Serves 1

4–5 ice cubes

1 measure pineapple juice

1 measure fresh lemon juice

1 measure fresh orange juice

½ teaspoon grenadine

3 measures gin

To Decorate:

slice of pineapple

cocktail cherry

Alice Springs in Australia's Northern Territory is situated just south of the Tropic of Capricorn – a place where it is easy to work up a thirst. This fruity cocktail may go some way towards undermining the probably undeserved reputation that Australians have for drinking only ice-cold lager.

Alice Springs

Put the ice cubes into a cocktail shaker. Pour in the lemon juice, orange juice, grenadine and gin. Add the bitters and shake until a frost forms. Pour into a tall glass and top up with soda water. Decorate with a slice of orange and serve with straws.

🕐 Preparation time: 3 minutes

🍸 Serves 1

4–5 ice cubes

1 measure fresh lemon juice

1 measure fresh orange juice

½ teaspoon grenadine

3 measures gin

3 drops Angostura bitters

soda water, to top up

slice of orange, to decorate

Undoubtedly, it is politically incorrect to describe a cocktail as a 'lady's drink', but it is, nevertheless, true that the sweet concoctions known as juleps have always appealed especially to the 'fair sex'. This pale pink, cherry-flavoured cocktail is no exception – but it can be enjoyed by anyone with a sweet tooth and a long thirst.

Cherry Julep

Put the ice cubes into a cocktail shaker. Pour the lemon juice, sugar syrup, grenadine, cherry brandy, sloe gin and gin over the ice. Fill a highball glass with finely chopped ice. Shake the mixture until a frost forms, then strain it into the ice-filled glass. Decorate with lemon rind strips and serve.

🕑 Preparation time: 3 minutes

🍸 Serves 1

3–4 ice cubes

juice of ½ lemon

1 teaspoon sugar syrup (see page 12)

1 teaspoon grenadine

1 measure cherry brandy

1 measure sloe gin

2 measures gin

chopped ice

lemon rind strips, to decorate

This is a delicately balanced, sweet-sour cocktail. The orange liqueurs and coconut cream are both very sweet, while the lime juice and gin have a sour taste. Pineapple juice, which is sweet, but also has an astringent quality, provides the bridge between the two extremes.

Juliana Blue

Put some crushed ice into a blender and pour in the gin, Cointreau, blue Curaçao, pineapple and lime juices and cream of coconut. Blend at high speed for several seconds until the mixture has the consistency of soft snow. Put the ice cubes into a cocktail glass and strain the mixture on to them. Decorate with a pineapple slice and cocktail cherries. Serve with straws.

🕐 Preparation time: 3 minutes

🍸 Serves 1

crushed ice
1 measure gin
½ measure Cointreau
½ measure blue Curaçao
2 measures pineapple juice
½ measure fresh lime juice
1 measure cream of coconut
1–2 ice cubes
To Decorate:
slice of pineapple
cocktail cherries

Clear Skies Ahead *left*

Put the ice cubes into a cocktail shaker. Pour in the sugar syrup, lemon juice, grenadine, egg white and whisky. Shake until a frost forms, then pour into a chilled old-fashioned glass. Serve decorated with a cocktail parasol.

🕐 Preparation time: 3 minutes

🍸 Serves 1

4–5 ice cubes

½ teaspoon sugar syrup (see page 12)

juice of ½ lemon

½ teaspoon grenadine

1 egg white

2 measures whisky

'No cloud was in the sky.'
This has always been regarded as an omen of good fortune.

It took Margaret Mitchell nine years to research and write her massive best-selling novel Gone with the Wind. *In doing so, she created one of the world's great romantic heroes, Rhett Butler, whose scallywag charm was further enhanced when Hollywood heart-throb Clark Gable played the role in the blockbuster movie.*

153

Rhett Butler

Put the ice cubes into a cocktail shaker. Pour the Curaçao, Southern Comfort, lime juice and lemon juice over the ice and shake until a frost forms. Strain into a highball glass and top up with soda water. Decorate with the orange rind spiral.

🕐 Preparation time: 3 minutes

🍸 Serves 1

4–5 ice cubes

1 measure Curaçao

2 measures Southern Comfort

2 teaspoons fresh lime juice

2 teaspoons fresh lemon juice

soda water, to top up

orange rind spiral, to decorate

'Frankly, my dear, I don't give a damn', must be one of the most frequently misquoted lines of all time.

Havana Beach

Cut the ½ lime into 4 pieces, put them into a
blender or food processor with the pineapple juice,
rum and sugar and blend until smooth. Put the ice
into a hurricane glass or large goblet, pour in the
drink and top up with ginger ale. Decorate with
the lime slice and serve with straws.

½ lime

2 measures pineapple juice

1 measure white rum

1 teaspoon sugar

3–4 ice cubes

ginger ale, to top up

slice of lime, to decorate

🕐 Preparation time: 3 minutes

🍸 Serves 1

This refreshing drink is given a slightly sharp edge by the bitters and tart cranberry juice. A sweeter version, Purple Rum, is made with dark rum and black grape juice.

Pink Rum

Shake the bitters into a highball glass and swirl them around. Add the ice cubes, then pour in the rum, cranberry juice and soda water and serve decorated with a lime slice.

- Preparation time: 2 minutes
- Serves 1

3 drops Angostura bitters
3–4 ice cubes
2 measures white rum
2 measures cranberry juice
1 measure soda water
slice of lime, to decorate

This is a variation on the Zombie, a cocktail that, to be authentic, always contains all three types of rum, a liqueur and fruit juice.

Rum Christophe

Put the ice cubes into a mixing glass. Pour the lime or lemon juice, orange juice, pineapple juice, Curaçao, white and golden rums over the ice. Stir vigorously, then pour, without straining, into a tumbler. Top with the dark rum, stir gently and serve decorated with a lemon slice and a mint sprig.

🕐 Preparation time: 3 minutes

🍸 Serves 1

4–5 ice cubes

juice of 1 lime or lemon

juice of ½ orange

250 ml (8 fl oz) unsweetened
    pineapple juice

1 measure blue Curaçao

1 measure white rum

1 measure golden rum

½ measure dark rum

To Decorate:

slice of lemon

sprig of mint

Tobago Fizz

Put the ice cubes into a cocktail shaker. Pour the lime or lemon juice, orange juice, rum, cream and sugar syrup over the ice. Shake until a frost forms, then strain into a goblet. Top up with soda water and serve decorated with a slice or two of orange and a slice of strawberry on a cocktail stick and drink with straws.

🕐 Preparation time: 3 minutes
🍸 Serves 1

4–5 ice cubes
juice of ½ lime or lemon
juice of ½ orange
3 measures golden rum
1 measure single cream
½ teaspoon sugar syrup (see page 12)
soda water, to top up
To Decorate:
slice of orange
slice of strawberry

Grenada Cocktail *top*

Put the ice cubes into a mixing glass. Pour the orange juice, vermouth and rum over the ice, stir vigorously, then strain into a cocktail glass and decorate with small pieces of cinnamon stick.

🕐 Preparation time: 2 minutes
🍸 Serves 1

4–5 ice cubes
juice of ½ orange
1 measure sweet vermouth
3 measures golden or dark rum
small pieces of cinnamon stick, to
    decorate (optional)

Time has distanced the days when the Spanish Main was the highway for pirates, and their activities have acquired a gloss of romance. The mere name of this cocktail conjures up an image of gaudily dressed sailors, a tattered Jolly Roger flying overhead, sailing safely into their Jamaican port.

Port Antonio *bottom*

Spoon the grenadine into a chilled cocktail glass. Put the ice cubes into a mixing glass. Pour the lime juice and rum over the ice and stir vigorously then strain into the cocktail glass. Wrap the lime rind round the cocktail cherry, impale them with a cocktail stick and use to decorate the drink.

🕐 Preparation time: 2 minutes
🍸 Serves 1

½ teaspoon grenadine
4–5 ice cubes
1 measure fresh lime juice
3 measures white or
    golden rum
To Decorate:
lime rind
cocktail cherry

159

'Yo-ho-ho, and a bottle of rum', so goes the chorus of the pirates' song from Treasure Island.

Florida Keys

Put the crushed ice, rum, lime juice, passion fruit juice and cream in a blender and blend until smooth. Pour into a hurricane glass and decorate with a slice of lime and a cocktail cherry.

🕐 Preparation time: 3 minutes
🍸 Serves 1

4–5 crushed ice cubes
2 measures white rum
1 measure fresh lime juice
1 measure passion fruit juice
1 measure double cream
To Decorate:
slice of lime
cocktail cherry

St Lucia *left*

Put the ice cubes into a cocktail shaker. Pour the Curaçao, vermouth, orange juice, grenadine and rum over the ice. Shake until a frost forms, then pour, without straining, into a highball glass. To serve, decorate with an orange rind spiral and a cocktail cherry.

🕐 Preparation time: 3 minutes
🍸 Serves 1

4–5 ice cubes
1 measure Curaçao
1 measure dry vermouth
juice of ½ orange
1 teaspoon grenadine
2 measures white or
    golden rum
To Decorate:
orange rind spiral
cocktail cherry

Banana Royal

Put some crushed ice into a blender and add the coconut milk, pineapple juice, rum, cream and banana. Blend for 15–30 seconds until smooth and creamy. Pour into an old-fashioned glass and sprinkle with grated coconut.

🕐 Preparation time: 3 minutes
🍸 Serves 1

crushed ice
1½ measures coconut milk
3 measures pineapple juice
1½ measures golden rum
½ measure double cream
1 ripe banana
grated coconut, to decorate

161

El Dorado

Put the ice cubes into a cocktail shaker. Pour the rum, advocaat and crème de cacao over the ice and add the coconut. Shake until a frost forms, then strain into a chilled cocktail glass.

🕐 Preparation time: 3 minutes
🍸 Serves 1

4–5 ice cubes
1 measure white rum
1 measure advocaat
1 measure crème de cacao
2 teaspoons grated coconut

'Apart from cheese and tulips, the main product of Holland is advocaat, a drink made from lawyers.'

Miles out in the Pacific ocean, just south of the Tropic of Cancer, lie the paradise islands of Hawaii. Coconuts, oranges, pineapples and sugar cane just come naturally together to make this stunning cocktail.

Blue Hawaiian

Put some crushed ice into a blender and pour in the rum, blue Curaçao, pineapple juice and cream of coconut. Blend for 20–30 seconds. Pour into a chilled glass and decorate with a piece of pineapple.

crushed ice
1 measure white rum
½ measure blue Curaçao
2 measures pineapple juice
1 measure cream of coconut
pineapple wedge, to decorate

🕐 Preparation time: 2 minutes

🍸 Serves 1

Bombay Smash

Put half of the ice into a cocktail shaker. Add the rum, Malibu, pineapple juice, lemon juice and Cointreau. Shake to mix. Put the remaining ice into a tall glass and strain the cocktail over it. Decorate with the pineapple cubes and the slice of lemon and drink with a straw.

🕐 Preparation time: 3 minutes
🍸 Serves 1

5 crushed ice cubes
1 measure dark rum
1 measure Malibu
3 measures pineapple juice
2 teaspoons lemon juice
¼ measure Cointreau
To Decorate:
pineapple cubes
slice of lemon

> **Malibu**
> Malibu is a high-quality rum blended with coconut.

Florida Skies

Put some cracked ice in a tall glass. Pour the rum, lime juice and pineapple juice into a cocktail shaker. Shake lightly. Strain into the glass and top up with soda water. Decorate with the slice of lime or cucumber.

🕐 Preparation time: 3 minutes
🍸 Serves 1

3 cracked ice cubes
1 measure white rum
¼ measure fresh lime juice
½ measure pineapple juice
soda water, to top up
slice of lime or cucumber,
    to decorate

163

Beautiful Beth

Put the ice cubes into a cocktail shaker. Pour the rum, Malibu and Cointreau over the ice and shake until a frost forms. Strain into a hurricane glass and top up with chilled cola. Decorate with cocktail cherries speared on a cocktail stick.

🕐 Preparation time: 3 minutes
🍸 Serves 1

3–4 crushed ice cubes
1 measure light rum
1 measure Malibu
½ measure Cointreau
chilled cola, to top up
cocktail cherries, to decorate

'The only way they could improve upon Coca Cola ... is to put rum or bourbon into it.'

Frozen Pineapple Daiquiri

Put some crushed ice into a blender and add the pineapple slices, lime juice, white rum, Cointreau and sugar syrup. Blend at the highest speed until smooth, then pour into a chilled cocktail glass. Decorate with a piece of pineapple and serve with a straw.

🕐 Preparation time: 2 minutes

🍸 Serves 1

crushed ice

2–3 slices of pineapple

½ measure fresh lime juice

1 measure white rum

¼ measure Cointreau

1 teaspoon sugar syrup (see
   page 12)

piece of pineapple,
   to decorate

'That frozen concoction
that helps me hang on.'

Apricot Daiquiri

Put some crushed ice into a blender. Add the rum, lemon juice, apricot liqueur or brandy and the apricots and blend for 1 minute or until the mixture is smooth. Pour into a chilled cocktail glass and decorate with an apricot slice, cocktail cherry and mint sprig.

🕐 Preparation time: 2 minutes
🍸 Serves 1

crushed ice
1 measure white rum
1 measure fresh lemon juice
½ measure apricot liqueur
    or brandy
3 ripe apricots, skinned
    and pitted
To Decorate:
slice of apricot
cocktail cherry
sprig of mint

Melon Daiquiri

Put the crushed ice into a cocktail shaker. Pour the rum, Midori and lime juice over the ice and shake until a frost forms. Strain into a chilled cocktail glass and decorate with a slice of lime.

🕐 Preparation time: 3 minutes
🍸 Serves 1

4–5 crushed ice cubes
2 measures white rum
2 measures Midori
1 measure fresh lime juice
slice of lime, to decorate

165

Midori
Midori is a Japanese liqueur made from melons.

Coconut Daiquiri

Put the crushed ice into a cocktail shaker. Pour the rum, coconut liqueur, lime juice and grenadine over the ice and shake until a frost forms. Strain into a cocktail glass and decorate with a slice of lime.

🕐 Preparation time: 3 minutes
🍸 Serves 1

4–5 crushed ice cubes
2 measures white rum
1 measure coconut liqueur
2 measures fresh lime juice
1 teaspoon grenadine
slice of lime, to decorate

Banana Daiquiri *left*

Put the cracked ice in a margarita glass or tall goblet. Put the rum, banana liqueur, banana and lime cordial into a blender and blend for 30 seconds. Pour into the glass and decorate with the powdered sugar, if using, and a slice of banana.

🕐 Preparation time: 2 minutes

🍸 Serves 1

3 ice cubes, cracked
2 measures white rum
½ measure banana liqueur
½ small banana
½ measure lime cordial
To Decorate:
1 teaspoon powdered
 sugar (optional)
slice of banana

This daiquiri is particularly delicious if you make it with crème de fraises des bois, a liqueur flavoured with wild strawberries. Decorate with a whole wild strawberry, too.

Strawberry Daiquiri *right*

Put the cracked ice in a margarita glass or tall goblet. Put the rum, strawberry liqueur and lime cordial into a blender and blend for 30 seconds. Pour into the glass and decorate with the powdered sugar, if using, and a slice of strawberry.

🕐 Preparation time: 2 minutes

🍸 Serves 1

4–5 cracked iced cubes
1 measure white rum
½ measure strawberry liqueur
½ measure lime cordial
To Decorate:
1 teaspoon powdered
 sugar (optional)
slice of strawberry

Telford

Put the ice cubes into a cocktail shaker. Pour the white rum, dark rum, tequila, Cointreau, apricot brandy, orange juice, bitters and grenadine over the ice and shake until a frost forms. Strain into a cocktail glass and decorate with cocktail cherries.

🕐 Preparation time: 3 minutes

🍸 Serves 1

4–5 ice cubes
1 measure white rum
1 measure dark rum
½ measure tequila
½ measure Cointreau
1 measure apricot brandy
1 measure fresh orange juice
2–3 drops orange bitters
dash of grenadine
cocktail cherries, to decorate

Mai Tai *left*

Dip the rim of a tall glass into the beaten egg white, then in the caster sugar. Put the rum, orange juice and lime juice into a cocktail shaker. Shake to mix. Put the ice into the glass and pour the cocktail over it. Decorate with the cherries, pineapple, and slices of orange and drink with a straw.

- Preparation time: 3 minutes
- Serves 1

lightly beaten egg white
caster sugar, for frosting
1 measure white rum
½ measure fresh orange juice
½ measure fresh lime juice
3 crushed ice cubes
To Decorate:
cocktail cherries
pineapple cubes
slices of orange

The idea of pirates making cocktails, rather than swigging their rum neat, owes more to Hollywood movies of the black-and-white era than to reality. Nevertheless, this concoction evokes a delightful picture of the First Mate, eye patch in place, wielding a cocktail shaker more in the style of Tom Cruise than Errol Flynn.

169

Jolly Roger

Put half of the ice cubes into a cocktail shaker. Add the rum, Galliano, apricot brandy and orange juice. Shake to mix. Put the remaining ice into a tall glass and strain the cocktail over it . Decorate with the slices of apricot, orange and lemon.

- Preparation time: 3 minutes
- Serves 1

5 ice cubes, cracked
1 measure dark rum
1 measure Galliano
½ measure apricot brandy
3 measures fresh orange juice
To Decorate:
slice of apricot
slice of orange
slice of lemon

Planter's Cocktail

Put the ice cubes into a cocktail shaker and add the rum, orange juice, lemon juice, bitters and sugar. Shake until a frost forms. Strain into a cocktail glass. Decorate with the pineapple, banana and spiral of orange.

- Preparation time: 3 minutes
- Serves 1

3 ice cubes, cracked
1 measure dark rum
½ measure fresh orange juice
½ measure fresh lemon juice
2 dashes Angostura bitters
1 teaspoon powdered sugar
To Decorate:
pineapple cubes
slices of banana
orange rind spiral

Coco Loco *left*

Pour the rum, tequila, vodka, coconut cream, lemon juice and ice cubes into a blender. Mix for 15 seconds. Pour into a large goblet or tall glass. Decorate with lemon spirals and sit the cherries on top. Drink with a straw.

🕐 Preparation time: 3 minutes
🍸 Serves 1

¾ measure white rum
¾ measure tequila
½ measure vodka
1 measure coconut cream
1 tablespoon fresh lemon juice
3 ice cubes, cracked
To Decorate:
spirals of lemon rind
1–2 cocktail cherries

Tropical Dream *right*

Pour the white rum, Midori, coconut cream, pine-apple and orange juices and the ice cubes into a blender. Mix for about 10 seconds. Add the crème de banane and the banana and mix for a further 10 seconds. Pour into a tall glass, decorate with the wedge of banana and drink with a straw.

🕐 Preparation time: 3 minutes
🍸 Serves 1

1 measure white rum
1 measure Midori
1 tablespoon coconut cream
3 tablespoons pineapple juice
3 tablespoons fresh orange juice
3–4 ice cubes
½ measure crème de banane
½ banana
wedge of fresh banana, with skin on, to decorate

Hummingbird

Put the ice cubes into a cocktail shaker. Pour the dark and light rums, Southern Comfort and orange juice over the ice and shake until a frost forms. Strain into a long glass and top up with cola. Decorate with a slice of orange and serve with a straw.

🕐 Preparation time: 3 minutes
🍸 Serves 1

4–5 crushed ice cubes
1 measure dark rum
1 measure light rum
1 measure Southern Comfort
1 measure fresh orange juice
cola, to top up
slice of orange, to decorate

'In the world where the humming-bird flashed ahead of creation.'

East India

Put the ice cubes into a mixing glass. Shake the bitters over the ice and add the pineapple juice. Pour in the Curaçao and brandy and stir vigorously, then strain into a chilled cocktail glass. Decorate with an orange rind spiral.

🕐 Preparation time: 2 minutes
🍸 Serves 1

4–5 ice cubes
3 drops Angostura bitters
½ measure pineapple juice
½ measure blue Curaçao
2 measures brandy
orange rind spiral, to decorate

'Once did she hold
the gorgeous east in fee.'

Morning

Put the ice into a mixing glass. Pour the bitters, Pernod, grenadine, vermouth, Curaçao and brandy over the ice and stir well. Strain into a chilled cocktail glass. Decorate with cocktail cherries.

🕐 Preparation time: 2 minutes

🍸 Serves 1

4–5 ice cubes

3 drops Angostura bitters

5 drops of Pernod

½ teaspoon grenadine

½ teaspoon dry vermouth

1 measure Curaçao

3 measures brandy

cocktail cherries, to decorate

''Tis always morning
somewhere in the world.'

Creole describes a marvellous cultural and linguistic melting pot of Spanish, French, African and American located in Louisiana and focused on New Orleans.

Creole Punch *left*

Put half of the ice into a cocktail shaker and add the port, brandy and lemon juice. Shake until a frost forms. Put the remaining ice into a hurricane glass or large goblet, pour the cocktail over it and top up with lemonade. Decorate with the fruit.

🕐 Preparation time: 3 minutes
🍸 Serves 1

5 ice cubes, crushed
1½ measures port
½ measure brandy
2 teaspoons fresh lemon juice
lemonade, to top up
To Decorate:
slice of orange
slice of lemon
cocktail cherries
slice of kiwi fruit

Leo

Put half the ice cubes into a cocktail shaker. Add the brandy, Amaretto and orange juice. Shake well. Strain into a tall glass filled with the remaining ice. Pour over the Campari and top up with soda water.

🕐 Preparation time: 3 minutes
🍸 Serves 1

6 ice cubes, crushed
1 measure brandy
½ measure Amaretto di Saronno
1½ measures fresh orange juice
1 teaspoon Campari
soda water, to top up

175

'Leo is a fiercely loyal friend, a just but powerful enemy, creative and original, strong and vital.'

Gypsy's Warning

Put the ice into a cocktail shaker. Pour the brandy, slivovitz and lemon juice over the ice and shake until a frost forms. Strain into a cocktail glass and decorate with a slice of orange and cocktail cherry.

🕐 Preparation time: 3 minutes
🍸 Serves 1

4–5 crushed ice cubes
1 measure brandy
1 measure slivovitz
1 measure fresh lemon juice
To Decorate:
slice of orange
cocktail cherry

Haven

Put the ice cubes into an old-fashioned glass. Dash the grenadine over the ice, then pour in the Pernod and vodka. Top up with soda water and serve with a straw.

🕐 Preparation time: 2 minutes

🍸 Serves 1

2–3 ice cubes
1 tablespoon grenadine
1 measure Pernod
1 measure vodka
soda water, to top up

This Oscar-winning cocktail can certainly take a starring role, but was the drink named to commemorate Sam Mendes' award-winning film or – surely much more likely – was he inspired to make a movie after drinking an American Beauty?

American Beauty

Put the ice cubes into a cocktail shaker and pour in the brandy, vermouth, orange juice, grenadine and crème de menthe. Shake well and strain into a cocktail glass. Tilt the glass and gently pour in a little ruby port so that it floats on top. Decorate with a cocktail cherry, orange slice and mint sprig on a cocktail stick.

🕐 Preparation time: 3 minutes

🍸 Serves 1

4–5 ice cubes
1 measure brandy
1 measure dry vermouth
1 measure fresh orange juice
1 measure grenadine
1 dash crème de menthe
ruby port
To Decorate:
cocktail cherry
slice of orange
mint sprig

When vodka was first produced, it was usually flavoured with herbs, spices or fruit, mainly to disguise its often filthy taste as it was produced from rotting potatoes and both controlled distillation and filtration were many centuries away. Modern vodka, in the West at least, has reached such a point of purification, it has no flavour at all. Recent years have seen a reversal of this pattern and nowadays vodkas flavoured with just about everything imaginable have become extremely fashionable as shots. Usually they are not suitable for making cocktails, but this is an exception.

PDQ

Put the ice cubes into a cocktail shaker. Pour the vodkas, bouillon and lemon juice over the ice and dash in the Tabasco and Worcestershire sauces. Shake until a frost forms, then strain into a hurricane glass. Season to taste with salt and pepper and decorate with a slice of lemon and a chilli.

- 🕐 Preparation time: 3 minutes
- 🍸 Serves 1

4–5 ice cubes
1½ measures chilli-
  flavoured vodka
1 measure vodka
2 measures chilled
  beef bouillon
1 tablespoon fresh lemon juice
dash of Tabasco sauce
dash of Worcestershire sauce
salt and black pepper
To Decorate:
slice of lemon
bottled chilli

178

Lime Gin Fizz *right*

Put the ice cubes into a tall glass. Pour the gin and the lime cordial over the ice cubes. Top up with soda water, decorate with wedges of lime and serve with straws.

- 🕐 Preparation time: 2 minutes
- 🍸 Serves 1

4–5 ice cubes
2 measures gin
1 measure lime cordial
soda water, to top up
lime wedges, to decorate

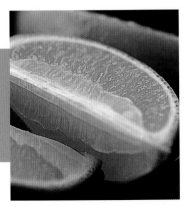

Lime wedges
Limes are an indispensable ingredient in many cocktails, both for their juice and as a decoration.

Melon Ball *left*

Pour the vodka, Midori and orange juice into a cocktail shaker. Shake well to mix. Put the cracked ice cubes into a tall glass or goblet and strain over the cocktail. Pour in the orange juice, adding more to top up, if necessary. Decorate with the fruit and drink with a straw.

1 measure vodka

1 measure Midori

1 measure fresh orange juice

5 ice cubes, cracked

To Decorate:

slice of oranges

small ball of banana

🕐 Preparation time: 3 minutes

🍸 Serves 1

This cocktail was a result of a serendipity, when, in 1941, an employee of a soft drinks company and a bar owner in Los Angeles put their heads together to work out what could be done with an over-stock of ginger beer.

Moscow Mule *right*

Put the cracked ice into a cocktail shaker. Add the vodka and lime juice. Shake until a frost forms. Pour into a hurricane glass or large tumbler. Top up with ginger beer. Decorate with a slice of lime and drink with a straw.

3–4 ice cubes, cracked

2 measures vodka

juice of 2 limes

ginger beer, to top up

slice of lime, to decorate

🕐 Preparation time: 3 minutes

🍸 Serves 1

Delft Donkey

Put the cracked ice into a cocktail shaker. Add the gin and lemon juice. Shake until a frost forms. Pour into a hurricane glass or large tumbler. Top up with ginger beer. Decorate with a slice of lemon and drink with a straw.

3–4 ice cubes, cracked

2 measures gin

juice of 1 lemon

ginger beer, to top up

slice of lemon, to decorate

🕐 Preparation time: 3 minutes

🍸 Serves 1

Exotic Cocktails

This cocktail has changed over the years as tequila has become better known outside its native Mexico. It was originally made with dark rum and did not include fruit juices. There are now a number of variations made with other spirits as the base, too.

Acapulco

Put some crushed ice into a cocktail shaker and pour in the tequila, rum, pineapple juice, grapefruit juice and coconut milk. Shake the drink, then pour it into a hurricane glass and decorate with a wedge of pineapple. Serve with straws.

🕐 Preparation time: 3 minutes

🍸 Serves 1

crushed ice
1 measure tequila
1 measure white rum
2 measures pineapple juice
1 measure fresh grapefruit juice
1 measure coconut milk
pineapple wedge, to decorate

Frozen Strawberry

Put some crushed ice into a blender and pour in the tequila, strawberry liqueur and lemon juice. Drop in the strawberries and blend for a few seconds. Pour, without straining, into a cocktail glass and decorate with a strawberry.

crushed ice
1 measure tequila
1 measure strawberry liqueur
dash of fresh lemon juice
4 ripe strawberries
fresh strawberry, to decorate

🕐 Preparation time: 2 minutes
🍸 Serves 1

Coconut Tequila

Put some crushed ice into a blender and add the tequila, lemon juice, coconut milk and maraschino. Blend for a few seconds, then pour into a highball glass and decorate with a lemon slice.

crushed ice
1 measure tequila
½ measure fresh lemon juice
½ measure coconut milk
3 dashes of maraschino
slice of lemon, to decorate

🕐 Preparation time: 2 minutes
🍸 Serves 1

183

Beckoning Lady

Fill a hurricane or highball glass with ice. Add the tequila and passion fruit juice and stir well to mix. Float the Galliano on top in a layer about 1 cm (½ inch) deep and decorate with cocktail cherries.

6–8 ice cubes
2 measures tequila
125 ml (4 fl oz) passion
    fruit juice
1–2 teaspoons Galliano
cocktail cherries, to decorate

🕐 Preparation time: 2 minutes
🍸 Serves 1

'Who is this lady who is forever beckoning? ... Some say that she is Love, or Dame Fortune. Some, honour in the field. Some the Muse herself ... But all I can tell you for certain is that her eyes are laughing, and that she is without mercy.'*

Siamese Slammer *right*

Put the vodka, orange juice, papaya, banana, lime juice and sugar syrup into a food processor and blend until smooth. Put the ice cubes into tall glasses, pour in the drink and decorate the glasses with papaya slices.

🕐 Preparation time: 5 minutes
🍸 Serves 4

125 ml (4 fl oz) vodka
juice of 2 oranges
1 small ripe papaya, peeled and chopped
1 banana, sliced
juice of 1 lime
125 ml (4 fl oz) sugar syrup (see page 12)
ice cubes
slices of papaya, to decorate

'We are Siamese, if you please, if you please, / We are Siamese, if you don't please.'

Thai Sunrise *left*

Put all the ingredients into a food processor and blend until the ice is crushed. Pour into tall glasses and decorate with a lime and orange slices and sprigs of mint.

🕐 Preparation time: 3 minutes
🍸 Serves 4

2 ripe mangoes, peeled and sliced
125 ml (4 fl oz) tequila
50 ml (2 fl oz) Cointreau
25 ml (1 fl oz) grenadine
75 ml (3 fl oz) fresh lime or lemon juice
75 ml (3 fl oz) sugar syrup (see page 12)
6 ice cubes, cracked
To Decorate:
slices of lime and orange
sprigs of mint

185

'Translated literally, Thailand means land of the free.'

Caribbean Champagne

right

Pour the rum, crème de banane and bitters into a chilled champagne flute. Top up with Champagne and stir gently. Decorate with the banana, pineapple and cherry, all speared on a cocktail stick.

🕐 Preparation time: 4 minutes
🍸 Serves 1

1 tablespoon light rum
1 tablespoon crème de banane
dash Angostura bitters
chilled Champagne or sparkling
   wine
To Decorate:
slice of banana
slice of pineapple
cocktail cherry

'I hate champagne more than anything in the world next to Seven-Up.'

Cheshire Cat

Put the ice cubes into a mixing glass. Pour the brandy, sweet vermouth and orange juice over the ice and stir to mix. Strain into a champagne flute and top up with Champagne. Squeeze the zest from the orange rind over the drink and decorate with an orange rind spiral.

🕐 Preparation time: 2 minutes
🍸 Serves 1

4–5 ice cubes
1 measure brandy
1 measure sweet vermouth
1 measure fresh orange juice
Champagne, to top up
orange rind strip
orange rind spiral, to decorate

'It vanished quite slowly, beginning with the end of the tail, and ending with the grin, which remained some time after the rest of it had gone.' This is a fairly accurate description of how to drink this cocktail – quite slowly until your grin is all that remains.

Zombie *left*

Place a hurricane glass or tall glass in the freezer until the outside becomes frosted. Put the ice into a cocktail shaker, add the rums, apricot brandy, fruit juices and sugar. Shake until a frost forms. Pour into the glass without straining. To decorate, spear the cherry and pineapple on to a cocktail stick and place across the top of the glass. Add the mint sprig and sprinkle the powdered sugar over the drink, if liked, and drink with a straw.

🕐 Preparation time: 3 minutes
🍸 Serves 1

3 ice cubes, cracked
1 measure dark rum
1 measure white rum
½ measure apricot brandy
2 measures pineapple juice
1 tablespoon fresh lime juice
2 teaspoons powdered sugar
To Decorate:
cocktail cherry
pineapple wedge
sprig of mint
powdered sugar (optional)

New Orleans Dandy

Put the ice cubes into a cocktail shaker. Pour the rum, peach brandy, orange juice and lime juice over the ice and shake until a frost forms. Strain into a champagne flute or tall glass and top up with Champagne.

🕐 Preparation time: 3 minutes
🍸 Serves 1

4–5 ice cubes
1 measure white rum
½ measure peach brandy
dash of fresh orange juice
dash of fresh lime juice
Champagne, to top up

189

Flaming Lamborghini

Pour the Kahlúa into a warmed cocktail glass. Gently pour half a measure of Sambuca over the back of a spoon into the cocktail glass to create two layers. Pour the Bailey's and blue Curaçao into shot glasses. Pour the remaining Sambuca into a warmed wine glass and carefully set the Sambuca alight with a match. Pour into the cocktail glass with care. Pour the Bailey's and Curaçao together into the lighted cocktail glass. Drink with a straw and enjoy.

🕐 Preparation time: 8 minutes
🍸 Serves 1

1 measure Kahlúa
1 measure Sambuca
1 measure Bailey's Irish Cream
1 measure blue Curaçao

There are those who believe that 1999 was the last year of the old millennium and 2000 was the first year of the new one. There are others, with an equally strong conviction that the old millennium did not end until 2000 was over and that 2001 marked the beginning of the new one. Controversy has raged, but surely it would have been better to celebrate the new millennium twice with this special cocktail?

Millennium Cocktail *right*

Put the ice cubes into a cocktail shaker, add the vodka, raspberry and orange juice and shake thoroughly. Strain into a champagne glass and pour in the chilled Champagne.

4–5 ice cubes
1 measure vodka
1 measure fresh raspberry juice
1 measure fresh orange juice
4 measures Champagne or
    sparkling dry white wine

🕐 Preparation time: 3 minutes
🍸 Serves 1

'Tomorrow'll be the happiest time of all the glad New Year.'

E = mc^2

Put the crushed ice into a cocktail shaker. Pour the Southern Comfort, lemon juice and maple syrup over the ice and shake until a frost forms. Strain into a champagne flute and top up with Champagne. Decorate with a strip of lemon rind.

4–5 crushed ice cubes
2 measures Southern Comfort
1 measure fresh lemon juice
½ measure maple syrup
Champagne, to top up
lemon rind, to decorate

🕐 Preparation time: 3 minutes
🍸 Serves 1

'The Restaurant at the End of the Universe is one of the most extraordinary ventures in the entire history of catering.' Sadly, author Douglas Adams has failed to provide the recipe for a Pan Galactic Gargle Blaster.*

Alcohol-free Cocktails

There is absolutely no reason why alcohol-free cocktails shouldn't be just as delicious and as exotic as any of those that contain the demon drink, and this chapter gives you a choice of some of the best. So whether you're under-age, driving, on the wagon or you simply don't drink alcohol, try some of these. Run up a jug of long Cool Passion or Tenderberry, or sip a few glasses of Cranberry Crush or Midsummer Punch, and chill out. You can drink all night long!

Carrot Cream *right*

Put the carrot juice, cream, egg yolks and orange juice into a cocktail shaker and shake well. Divide the ice cubes among 4 tall glasses and pour the carrot drink on top. Decorate with orange slices and serve immediately. Serve with straws.

🕐 Preparation time: 5 minutes
🍸 Serves 4

250 ml (8 fl oz) carrot juice
300 ml (½ pint) single cream
4 egg yolks
125 ml (4 fl oz) fresh orange juice
20 ice cubes
slices of orange, to decorate

San Francisco *left*

Put the ice cubes into a cocktail shaker and pour in the orange, lemon, pineapple and grapefruit juices, grenadine and egg white. Shake well, then strain into a large goblet. Top up with soda water and decorate with the lemon and lime slices and cocktail cherry on a cocktail stick and an orange rind spiral. Serve with a straw.

🕐 Preparation time: 3 minutes
🍸 Serves 1

3 ice cubes
1 measure fresh orange juice
1 measure fresh lemon juice
1 measure pineapple juice
1 measure fresh grapefruit juice
2 dashes of grenadine
1 egg white
soda water, to top up
To Decorate:
slice of lemon
slice of lime
cocktail cherry
orange rind spiral

195

All Shook Up

Put the berries, milk, yogurt and rosewater in a blender and blend until smooth. Pour into a tall glass and stir in the honey. Decorate with slices of strawberry.

🕐 Preparation time: 2 minutes
🍸 Serves 1

50 g (2 oz) mixed strawberries and raspberries
125 ml (4 fl oz) chilled milk
125 ml (4 fl oz) chilled natural yogurt
1 teaspoon rosewater
½ teaspoon clear honey
slices of strawberry, to decorate

Grapefruit Mint Cooler

Put the sugar and water into a heavy-based saucepan and stir over a low heat until dissolved. Leave to cool. Crush the mint leaves and stir them into the syrup. Cover and leave to stand for about 12 hours, then strain into a jug. Add the lemon and grapefruit juices to the strained syrup and stir well. Fill 6 old-fashioned glasses or tumblers with crushed ice and pour the cocktail into the glasses. Pour in the soda water and decorate with mint sprigs.

125 g (4 oz) sugar
125 ml (4 fl oz) water
handful of mint sprigs
juice of 4 large lemons
450 ml (¾ pint) fresh
    grapefruit juice
crushed ice
250 ml (8 fl oz) soda water
sprigs of mint, to decorate

🕐 Preparation time: 5 minutes, plus standing

🍸 Serves 6

Cool Passion

Pour the two fruit juices into a large jug. Stir
well to mix. Just before serving, stir in the lemonade. Pour into glasses containing a little crushed ice.

🕐 Preparation time: 2 minutes
🍸 Serves 20

500 ml (17 fl oz) carton orange and
    passion fruit juice
1 litre (1¾ pint) carton
    pineapple juice
1.5 litres (2½ pints) lemonade
crushed ice

Anita

Put the ice cubes into a cocktail shaker with the
orange juice, lemon juice and bitters and shake
well. Strain into a tumbler and top up with soda
water. Decorate with slices of lemon and orange.

🕐 Preparation time: 3 minutes
🍸 Serves 1

3 ice cubes
1 measure fresh orange juice
1 measure fresh lemon juice
3 dashes Angostura bitters
soda water, to top up
To Decorate:
slice of lemon
slice of orange

197

Brown Horny Toad

Put the ice cubes into a cocktail shaker. Pour in
the pineapple, orange and lemon juices, and the
grenadine and add the sugar syrup and spices.
Shake until a frost forms. Strain into a highball
glass and decorate with orange and lemon slices.

🕐 Preparation time: 3 minutes
🍸 Serves 1

4–5 crushed ice cubes
2 measures fresh
    pineapple juice
2 measures fresh orange juice
1 measure fresh lemon juice
1 tablespoon grenadine
1 teaspoon sugar syrup (see
    page 12)
pinch of ground cinnamon
pinch of ground cloves
To Decorate:
slice of orange
slice of lemon

'The clever men at Oxford
Know all that there is to be knowed
But they none of them know one half
    as much
As intelligent Mr Toad.'

Tenderberry *left*

Place the strawberries, grenadine and cream in a
food processor with some crushed ice and blend
for 30 seconds. Pour into a tumbler. Add the dry
ginger ale and stir. Sprinkle a little ground ginger
on top and decorate with a strawberry, if liked.

🕐 Preparation time: 4 minutes

🍸 Serves 1

6–8 strawberries
1 measure grenadine
1 measure double cream
crushed ice
1 measure dry ginger ale
a little ground ginger
1 whole strawberry, to
      decorate (optional)

Limeade *right*

Halve the limes, then squeeze the juice into a large
jug. Put the squeezed halves into a heatproof jug
with the sugar and boiling water and leave to infuse
for 15 minutes. Add the salt, give the infusion a
good stir, then strain it into the jug with the lime
juice. Add half a dozen ice cubes, cover and
refrigerate for 2 hours or until chilled. To serve,
place 3–4 ice cubes in each glass and pour the
limeade over them. Decorate with a lime wedge.

🕐 Preparation time: 5 minutes, plus infusing
and chilling

🍸 Serves 8

6 limes
125 g (4 oz) caster sugar
750 ml (1¼ pints) boiling water
pinch of salt
ice cubes
lime wedges, to decorate

199

Lime Juice
It is always better to use the juice of real limes in cocktails.

Caribbean Cocktail

Put the mango, banana, orange juice and lime in
a blender and blend until smooth. Put the ice into
2 highball glasses and pour the cocktail over it.
Decorate with slices of lime.

🕐 Preparation time: 2 minutes

🍸 Serves 2

1 mango, peeled and stoned
1 banana, peeled
juice of 1 large orange
dash of fresh lime juice
8–10 ice cubes
slices of lime, to decorate

Prohibition Punch

Stir together the sugar syrup, lemon and apple juices in a large chilled jug. Add the ice cubes and pour in the ginger ale. Decorate with orange slices and serve in tall glasses with straws.

🕐 Preparation time: 5 minutes

🍸 Serves 25–30

125 ml (4 fl oz) sugar syrup
  (see page 12)
350 ml (12 fl oz) fresh
  lemon juice
900 ml (1½ pints) apple juice
ice cubes
2.4 litres (4 pints) ginger ale

Café Astoria

Place the coffee essence, milk, pineapple juice and lemon juice in a blender with the ice and blend on maximum speed for 30 seconds. Pour into a cocktail glass and sprinkle the shavings of chocolate on top just before serving.

🕐 Preparation time: 2 minutes

🍸 Serves 1

1½ measures coffee essence
2 measures milk
¼ measure pineapple juice
¼ measure fresh lemon juice
3 ice cubes, crushed
shavings of chocolate,
   to decorate

'Coffee, which makes the politician wise ...' Perhaps politicians were different in Alexander Pope's day – or, perhaps, they have just stopped drinking coffee.

Nairobi Night

Pour the coffee into a bowl and stir in the sugar. Set aside to cool. Whisk together the cream and ice cream, then beat into the coffee. Continue beating until smooth and frothy. Pour into a jug and chill in the refrigerator for 1 hour, stirring occasionally. To serve, pour into 2 large goblets and float the ice cubes on top.

🕐 Preparation time: 5 minutes, plus cooling and chilling

🍸 Serves 2

450 ml (¾ pint) freshly
   made coffee
2 tablespoons caster sugar
4 tablespoons single cream
150 ml (¼ pint) vanilla
   ice cream
4 ice cubes

Bitter Sweet

Put the crushed ice into a cocktail shaker, pour over 3 tablespoons of the mineral water and the bitters and add the mint leaves. Shake until a frost forms. Pour into chilled glasses, top up with the remaining mineral water and decorate each glass with a slice of lemon or lime.

🕐 Preparation time: 3 minutes

🍸 Serves 4

crushed ice
600 ml (1 pint) sparkling mineral
   water, chilled
8 dashes of Angostura bitters
handful of fresh mint leaves
slices of lemon or lime,
   to decorate

Cranberry Crush *left*

Place the cranberry and orange juices, water, ginger and mixed spice in a saucepan and bring gently to the boil, stirring in sugar to taste. Simmer for 5 minutes. Pour into punch cups, decorate with kumquats, frosted cranberries and mint sprigs. Serve this drink hot in the winter and chilled for a summer party.

🕐 Preparation time: 10 minutes
🍸 Serves 10

600 ml (1 pint) cranberry juice
600 ml (1 pint) fresh orange juice
150 ml (¼ pint) water
½ teaspoon ground ginger
½ teaspoon mixed spice
sugar, to taste
To Decorate:
kumquats
frosted cranberries
mint sprigs

Fruit Punch *right*

Pour the orange, cranberry and pineapple juices and soda water into a large punch bowl or jug and mix well. Leave to chill in the refrigerator until required. To serve, add the ice cubes and decorate with the slices of orange and apple.

🕐 Preparation time: 5 minutes, plus chilling
🍸 Serves 12

600 ml (1 pint) fresh orange juice
600 ml (1 pint) cranberry juice
300 ml (½ pint) pineapple juice
250 ml (8 fl oz) soda water
ice cubes
To Decorate:
slices of orange
slices of apple

Tomato and Orange Cocktail

Put the tomato juice, oranges, cucumber, Worcestershire sauce and salt to taste in a blender and blend at high speed for 10–15 seconds. Strain into a jug and chill in the refrigerator. To serve, pour into 4 tall glasses and decorate with orange and cucumber slices.

🕐 Preparation time: 5 minutes
🍸 Serves 4

600 ml (1 pint) tomato juice
2 oranges, peeled and cut
    into 8 pieces
10 cm (4 inch) piece of cucumber,
    peeled and cut into 8 chunks
½ teaspoon Worcestershire
    sauce
salt
To Decorate:
4 slices of orange
4 slices of cucumber

Iced Mint Tea

Chop 4 of the mint sprigs and put them into a large heatproof jug with the lemon and sugar. Pour the tea into the jug and set the mixture aside to infuse for 20–30 minutes. Strain into another jug and chill in the refrigerator until required. To serve, pour into tumblers or tall glasses filled with ice and decorate each glass with slices of lemon and some of the remaining mint sprigs.

12 mint sprigs
1 lemon, finely chopped
1 tablespoon sugar
1.2 litres (2 pints) weak
    tea, strained
ice cubes
slices of lemon, to decorate

🕐 Preparation time: 5 minutes, plus infusing and chilling

🍸 Serves 4

Midsummer Punch

Put the sugar and water into a saucepan and stir until the sugar has dissolved. Leave to cool, then pour into a large jug or bowl. Stir in the fruit juices and cold tea, then add the sliced fruit and the crushed ice. To serve, pour into tall glasses and top up with ginger ale. Decorate with mint sprigs.

- Preparation time: 15 minutes
- Serves 8–10

125 g (4 oz) sugar
300 ml (½ pint) water
300 ml (½ pint) fresh orange juice
300 ml (½ pint) pineapple juice
600 ml (1 pint) cold weak tea, strained
slices of fruit (e.g. orange, lemon, apple and pineapple)
crushed ice
300 ml (½ pint) ginger ale
sprigs of mint, to decorate

Tropical Treat

Place the yogurt, pineapple and mineral water in a food processor or blender and process, in batches if necessary. Put the ice cubes into a tall jug, then pour in the drink through a very fine strainer. Stir, then add sugar to taste and stir again. To serve, pour into tall glasses and decorate with mint sprigs.

- Preparation time: 5 minutes
- Serves 4

900 ml (1½ pints) yogurt
1 large ripe pineapple, peeled and roughly chopped
300 ml (½ pint) sparkling mineral water
ice cubes
sugar, to taste
sprigs of mint, to decorate

River Cruise

Remove and discard any melon seeds. Put the flesh in a food processor or blender and process to a smooth purée. Transfer the purée to a large jug. Put the lemon rind and juice in a small saucepan with the sugar and stir over a low heat until dissolved. Strain the lemon mixture into the melon purée. Mix well, then stir
in the soda water. Chill in the refrigerator.

- Preparation time: 15 minutes, plus chilling
- Serves 4–6

500 g (1 lb) cantaloupe melon, peeled weight
rind and juice of 2 lemons
2 tablespoons sugar
600 ml (1 pint) soda water

'She's as headstrong as an allegory on the banks of the Nile'.

Index

Index

208

Picture acknowledgements in source order

Octopus Publishing Group Ltd./Sandra Lane 116
/Neil Mersh 26–27, 28, 29, 30 Bottom, 35, 36 Top, 37, 38, 40, 44, 46, 48, 51, 52, 54–55, 56, 58, 59, 60, 61, 65, 67, 68, 71, 72, 74, 75, 76, 77, 79, 83, 88, 88 Bottom, 92, 97, 98, 100, 101, 103, 106, 111, 112, 114-115, 117, 118, 122, 124, 126, 127, 128, 129, 130, 139, 141, 144, 145, 149, 152, 155, 156, 157, 167, 168, 171, 172, 174, 179, 181, 187, 188, 191, 194, 196, 200, 204
/Peter Myers/Neil Mersh 87, 154
/Bill Reavell Front Cover, Back Cover, 30 Top, 31, 33, 36 Bottom, 39, 41, 43, 53, 62, 63, 64, 80, 84, 85, 88 Top, 91, 93, 94, 96, 105, 108, 120, 123, 133, 134, 135, 137, 142–143, 147, 148, 150, 151, 158, 160, 162, 164, 173, 176, 177, 182, 184, 192–193, 198, 203
/Ian Wallace 42, 178, 199